THAMES AIRFIELDS IN THE SECOND WORLD WAR

Berkshire, Buckinghamshire
and Middlesex

CHRISTMAS 2000

TO DAD

HAPPY
CHRISTMAS
HOPE YOU
ENJOY THIS

PETER
xx

Robin J. Brooks

COUNTRYSIDE BOOKS
NEWBURY, BERKSHIRE

COUNTRYSIDE BOOKS
3 Catherine Road
Newbury, Berkshire

To view our complete range of books,
please visit us at
www.countrysidebooks.co.uk

ISBN 1 85306 633 8

The cover painting is from an original by
Colin Doggett and shows 303 Polish Squadron
departing Northolt in August 1940

Designed by Mon Mohan

Produced through MRM Associates Ltd., Reading
Printed by Woolnough Bookbinding Ltd., Irthlingborough

CONTENTS

THAMES VALLEY AIRFIELDS IN THE SECOND WORLD WAR

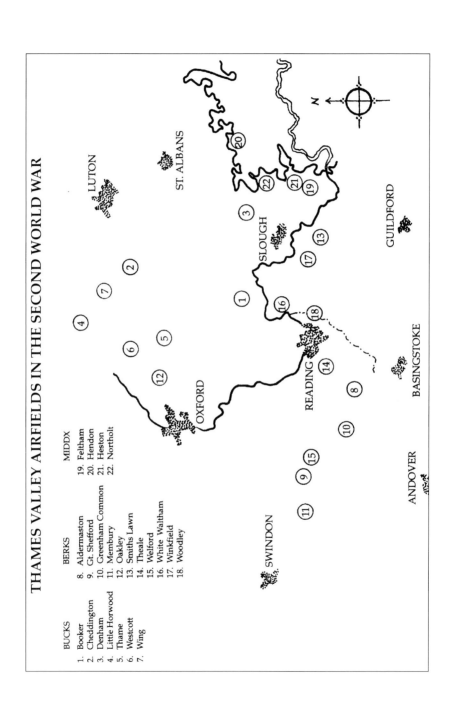

BUCKS
1. Booker
2. Cheddington
3. Denham
4. Little Horwood
5. Thame
6. Westcott
7. Wing

BERKS
8. Aldermaston
9. Gt. Shefford
10. Greenham Common
11. Membury
12. Oakley
13. Smiths Lawn
14. Theale
15. Welford
16. White Waltham
17. Winkfield
18. Woodley

MIDDX
19. Feltham
20. Hendon
21. Heston
22. Northolt

The Air Transport Auxiliary, White Waltham. A Stirling bomber dwarfs its pilot, Flt Capt Joan Hughes. An outstanding woman aviator, she joined the ATA in January 1940, at the age of 21. She became the only woman pilot to instruct on all classes of aircraft and delivered 75 four-engined bombers herself. After the war she remained as a flying instructor at White Waltham until 1961. She died in 1993. (Photo courtesy of West London Aero Club)

INTRODUCTION

Though some distance from the Channel coast and therefore from the main battle area, the airfields of Berkshire, Buckinghamshire and Middlesex none the less played a vital part in the war effort. Heston, Hendon and Northolt in Middlesex were in the thick of the Battle of Britain with all three airfields encompassed within No 11 Group of Fighter Command. The valiant Polish squadrons spent a lot of their time flying from Heston and Northolt, their unfailing patriotism and hatred of the enemy spurring them on to fight harder. Just a short distance away, the airfields of Berkshire and Buckinghamshire were mainly used in the training and troop carrying roles. In the latter, it was the USAAF that arrived to carry out much of this sterling work. From bases such as Aldermaston and Greenham Common, vast armies were carried in troop carrying aircraft and gliders to begin the assault on mainland Europe that would eventually bring victory. For the RAF, many bomber Operational Training Units were stationed within the region ensuring that Bomber Command always had a surplus of crews. It was also a time when the skies above the Thames Valley were filled with the roar of aircraft engines.

The civilian population of the three counties also came to see war at its most devastating with bombing raids on most of the towns at one time or another. Though away from the Channel coast, they were to suffer some dreadful attacks with civilian deaths and injuries. They all incurred scars upon their memories that time will never erase.

In this volume I have attempted to bring to the reader the feel of that time. The units that flew from the airfields, the death and destruction and the horror of war are all recorded. In this respect, I dedicate the following pages to all those that died or suffered through those traumatic times.

Robin J. Brooks

I
SETTING
THE SCENE

If the First World War had established the importance of aviation, the peace that followed almost broke the new industry. Now that the conflict was over, Europe, including Great Britain, found itself nearly bankrupt. It was only the dream of popular and commercial flying that kept the industry alive.

It was a series of pioneering flights from 1930 onwards that once again brought aviation into the headlines. Among the several people responsible for this new interest was Amy Johnson who in 1930, flew from Croydon to Australia. That same year saw Alan Cobham, back from one of his own long distance flights, beginning to entertain a whole new audience with his Flying Circus and National Aviation Day Tours. In 1932, many sites within the Thames Valley region were visited: Reading, Stag Lane, High Wycombe, Bletchley and many others. Again in 1933, Cobham visited Newbury, Uxbridge and Maidenhead, each time bringing aviation back to the people.

By the time that a certain unrest was beginning to show in Germany once again, the public were taking aircraft and aviation in their stride. It was lucky they did for with just 27 military and 17 civil airfields in the whole of Great Britain, the country was once again unprepared for war.

Among the military leaders at the time, one man had the foresight to see what was about to happen. Hugh Caswall Tremeneere Dowding was born on 24th April 1882 at Moffat in Dumfriesshire. After attending Winchester School, he entered the Royal Military Academy at Woolwich in September 1899. He served some of his time in Hong Kong and India and it was after six years at the latter that Dowding returned to attend the Staff College. By this time he had gradually become disillusioned with army life and it was during an exercise which was using aircraft for reconnaissance that he first felt his future lay in the newly formed Royal Flying Corps. This inspired him to apply for flying training and in 1913, he obtained his pilot's licence from the Royal Aero Club.

During the First World War he was to command several squadrons and with the signing of the armistice in 1918, he became one of the most senior officers in the newly formed Royal Air Force. By 1929, Dowding had reached the rank of Air Vice Marshal and by 1936 had become the first Commander-in-Chief of Fighter Command. At the same time, across the Channel, the Spanish Civil War had started. General Francisco Franco solicited help from both Italy and Germany, help that was readily given. For the Luftwaffe, restricted by the terms of the armistice, it was to be a proving ground for their planned conquest of the air above Europe.

It soon became obvious to Dowding and his Air Staff that a rapid expansion of the airforce was needed to compete with an ever increasing Luftwaffe. After a succession of various plans, named alphabetically, it was Scheme L that was finally approved by the Cabinet in April 1938. It contained roughly the same number of bombers as had been suggested for the previous scheme (around 1,360), but an increase in fighters from 532 to 600, these to receive priority building over the bombers. It was appreciated that the era of the biplane fighter had ended and that this new war that was threatening would be fought by highly powered monoplane aircraft, one of which was already on the drawing board by 1934.

The name of the Hawker Hurricane will forever be linked with the Battle of Britain. Though it was later to be joined by the Spitfire, during the months of July to October 1940, the Hurricane

9

Air Chief Marshal Sir Hugh Dowding, GCB, GCVO, CMG. Known as 'Stuffy', he was the AOC-in-C Fighter Command during the Battle of Britain. (IWM)

shot down more enemy aircraft than did all other defences, both air and ground. With the first aircraft in service by 1937, it began a new era of faster and more deadly aerial warfare. The Hurricane was also the first type to carry eight guns instead of the usual four. It first entered service, appropriately for this book, with No 111 Squadron at Northolt in December 1937 where it superseded the biplane Gloster Gauntlet. On the outbreak of war, some Hurricane squadrons were moved to France as part of the Advanced Air Striking Force but they were to return to the UK by April and May 1940 as the Germans advanced towards Dunkirk.

It had been hoped that these squadrons would forestall the German onslaught but the losses that they suffered could not be sustained. On 13th May 1940, a further 32 Hurricanes and pilots had been sent to France yet still the French Government demanded more. Dowding viewed this with grave doubts for he knew that when the time came to defend Britain, every aircraft and pilot would be needed here. He demanded an urgent meeting with Churchill and when this was approved, he placed a large graph in front of the Prime Minister and said: 'If the present wastage continues for another fortnight, we shall not have a

Had England been invaded, the Ju 52 troop carrier may well have been the first enemy aircraft to land on English soil. (MAP)

11

single Hurricane left in France or in this country.' Despite this plea, further orders were issued allocating four more fighter squadrons to the Continent. This time however, Cyril Newall, the Chief of the Air Staff, took a stand and allowed the squadrons to deploy to the forward airfields on the South Coast and no further. Thus they could fly over the Channel to defend France and then return to Britain. The change in policy could not have come at a more fortunate time.

For the Spitfire, production had begun at Supermarine in 1937. First deliveries were made to the RAF in June 1938 with No 19 Squadron at Duxford being the first to form. Its first claim to fame was on 16th October 1939 when two Spitfires shot down two Heinkel bombers, the first German aircraft to be shot down over Great Britain since 1918. By July 1940, there were 19 squadrons of Spitfires in Fighter Command in readiness for the Battle of Britain and during the period July to October, there were 957 Spitfires in service as against 1,326 Hurricanes. Though perhaps aesthetically more pleasing than the rugged Hurricane, the latter could receive and take more punishment before succumbing to destruction. It was, however, the Spitfire that has remained in most people's minds as the epitome of the Battle of Britain aircraft. Thus, it was with these two types plus two squadrons of the much maligned Boulton Paul Defiants, that Dowding and his commanders hoped to swing the tide of the battle in our favour.

With the new policy of aircraft requirements, the Air Ministry Works Directorate was formed and given responsibility for planning and overseeing the construction and expansion of new and existing airfields. Most were situated around London, ie Biggin Hill, Kenley, North Weald and Northolt. They were all grass and small with little in the way of facilities such as accommodation and hangarage. What there was usually consisted of canvas and was certainly not very strong. With Hitler's seizure of power in January 1933, the task ahead was critical and daunting, to say the least.

A few of the already constructed airfields were privately owned and were used for flying clubs and flying tuition. Others were permanent civil airfields used for scheduled flights, such as they were in the 1930s, whilst some had begun life as purely military.

Construction of an airfield 'somewhere in the South East'. The photo shows the laying of a hard runway. (IWM)

One of the latter airfields was Northolt in Middlesex, situated twelve miles west of central London and one of the sites constructed for the protection of the capital. Built to train pilots and observers for the Royal Flying Corps, it rapidly developed into a major airfield during the First World War. It survived the cutbacks between the wars and gradually began to be used more and more by civilian aircraft. Being the closest medium-sized airfield to London, it often acquired the title of London Airport. The Second World War saw it rapidly developed as a military airfield encompassed within No 11 Group of Fighter Command. It became home to many Polish squadrons during the six years of war and when peace finally came, it became a major transport airfield. Since that time, Northolt has survived all the reductions in military bases that have taken place under the guise of 'Options for Change'.

The only other fighter airfield in Middlesex was Heston. Developed solely for private flying, it opened in 1928. Situated just a few miles from Heston village, it quickly grew into a flying club, was used for aircraft production and was also a scheduled passenger airfield. It became a satellite to Northolt in 1940 and

The Nissen hut is still to be seen on many wartime airfields, including Northolt.

later in the war, was given squadron status. It reverted back to a satellite as the end of the war approached and was used as a civil airport in peacetime. The construction of the M4 motorway ensured it did not survive as an airfield but its one moment of fame was when Neville Chamberlain returned from his meeting with Hitler in Munich with a meaningless piece of paper in his hand.

Hendon today is world famous for the magnificent RAF Museum now covering the site. One of the best aeronautical museums in the world, it was established in 1963 and covers about ten acres of the former airfield. The early pioneer, Claude Grahame-White first used the site to test a Farman biplane in 1910 and is consequently forever associated with the airfield. He started a flying school with Hendon rapidly becoming known for air races during the early 1900s. The First World War saw the Grahame-White works producing aircraft for the services together with the establishment of a Royal Naval Air Service delivery centre for new aircraft. The armistice brought a return to

14

A formation of Do 215s en route to Britain. (MAP)

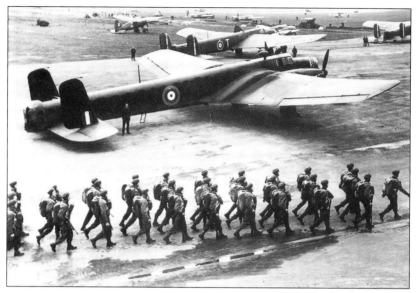

Practising for D-Day – troops ready to embark on Whitley bombers. Several Thames Valley airfields saw such scenes. (SE Newspapers)

civil use although the 1930s saw increased military use with the famous Hendon Air Displays, together with the further usage of the field by several RAF auxiliary squadrons. The outbreak of war brought Hendon once again into military hands as an airfield within No 11 Group of Fighter Command. Though not used as a pure fighter base, it served with distinction throughout the war and was used by the US Navy in peacetime. It closed for good in 1968, much of the site being used for housing. With its history, it certainly is an appropriate site for the RAF Museum.

With the planning and eventual execution of Operation Overlord, the Allied assault upon Fortress Europe, the county of Berkshire, too far away from the Battle of Britain counties, was mainly given over to the heavier units of the United States Army Air Force and flying training for the RAF. Many troop carrier groups were formed for the one purpose of a landing on enemy soil. The largest of these assaults, D-Day, saw many hundreds of DC3 Dakotas overhead, towing gliders which were full of troops, both American and British. With such great armadas of aircraft,

16

large airfields were required away from the main south coast battle area.

One of these airfields, Aldermaston, is nowadays renowned for a far more sinister type of warfare, nuclear. For wartime use, it was not chosen until 1941 as an operational training unit for bombers. The intended Wellingtons never arrived and the base was handed over to the USAAF for trooping movements. At the end of the war it was handed back to the RAF and used as a training base for BOAC. In 1950 it was converted to its present use, that of the Atomic Weapons Research Establishment.

Greenham Common on the other hand was used more extensively by the USAAF. Surveyed in 1941 as a possible satellite to the aforementioned Aldermaston, again this site was intended for the RAF but became a base for the Americans. Used by the heavier aircraft, Greenham Common gave sterling service over the D-Day period when C-47s (Dakotas) towing Hadrian and Horsa gliders, were some of the first aircraft over Normandy during 5th/6th June 1944. In 1945, the base was returned to the RAF and Technical Training Command but it quickly fell out of use when declared surplus to requirements. The Cold War of the 1950s brought a further American use of Greenham Common including the storage of Cruise missiles. The base became the subject of intense anti-nuclear campaigns but with the end of the Cold War in the early 1990s, the Americans left. Today it is in a state of disrepair and is again the subject of controversy concerning just what to do with it.

Membury was another site used by the USAAF though this time for reconnaissance aircraft. Again, intended as a bomber OTU, it was occupied by the Americans flying a diverse collection of aircraft such as Havocs, Mustangs and C-47s. Taken back by the RAF in 1947, it was used by Transport Command until it was decommissioned. Much of it today is industrial but parts of the original runways are still used for limited light flying.

The last of the USAAF bases in the county was Welford. Yet another bomber OTU, it was taken over by the USAAF for troop movements. Transport Command assumed responsibility for Welford in 1945 but it was reduced to Care and Maintenance a year later. Part of the site was reopened under Maintenance

Command but again reverted to Care and Maintenance in August 1952. Part of the site remains, neglected, today.

For the RAF, the county supported Great Shefford as a relief or emergency landing field but it saw little use. Theale was an RAF Elementary Training School using the standard trainer of the time, the Tiger Moth. It served its purpose throughout the war, only being placed under Care and Maintenance on 30th June 1945. An Air Cadet Gliding School remained until 1948 when it was decommissioned with part of the site becoming a gravel quarry.

The remaining Berkshire airfields were mainly used for training. Oakley was an RAF Flying Training Base, and Woodley which opened in 1939 served a similar role with the addition of the Miles Aircraft factory producing the Magister trainer. From 1946 until 1951, it was used as a communications base but all flying ceased in 1953. The site is now a housing estate. Finally in the county is Smith's Lawn. Originally a private landing strip, Vickers Armstrong used the field in 1940 for building special versions of the Wellington bomber. Situated in a corner of Windsor Great Park, it was a storage depot for Vickers Warwick bombers until the end of the war when it returned to its former use, that of a park.

In Buckinghamshire, the USAAF used Cheddington as a crew and aircraft replacement centre and a satellite airfield when it was found to be unsuitable for full operational use. RAF Operational Flying Training in the county was carried out at Booker, Little Horwood, Westcott and Wing with glider pilot training being carried out at Thame. Being too far from the main battle area, the Buckinghamshire airfields were mainly used for training.

So the scene was set for the Thames Valley airfields to go to war. Undoubtedly, Northolt, as the main fighter base was to suffer from the effects of war more than the rest but it must be said that without all the training bases, the others would not have received a ready supply of pilots or aircraft. A strong American presence brought home the fact that from 1942, we were not alone in fighting the enemy, although now, with the ending of the Cold War, that presence has virtually gone. Most of the airfields in the three counties are now part of history,

Northolt being the only visible reminder of times past. Let us hope that it remains so in these times of trouble in different parts of the world, lest we are once again, unprepared!

Balloon Command

Although usually associated only with the Second World War, the previous conflict had seen a limited use of the barrage balloon. The expansion of such an idea however gathered pace at roughly the same time as the accelerated expansion of the RAF. It was considered a fairly cheap method of defence and one that could certainly bring results in the downing of enemy aircraft. Even if this did not happen, the height at which they were intended to be flown, between 1,000 and 10,000 feet, would certainly deter enemy aircraft from flying low in order to hit a target. The one disadvantage however of such a defence was that sometimes our own aircraft flew into the barrage and were lost.

A partially deflated barrage balloon. The sites were widely dispersed around the countryside. (SE Newspapers)

19

It fell to two Royal Aircraft Establishment scientists, Ben Lockspeiser and Roxbee Cox to investigate the possibility of barrage balloons as a method of aerial defence. It was also their task to find out the effect on an aircraft when it did fly into the balloon wire, with early experiments being conducted by flying into string (actually nylon fishing line) dangling from a parachute. These experiments showed what even a soft substance such as nylon wire could do to the leading edge of a wing.

The aircraft used in the experiments was a Miles Hawk two-seat trainer. Once airborne, one of the men would throw the rolled up wire attached to a parachute overboard whereupon it would slowly open and the wire would unravel. The aircraft would then level up and fly directly into the wire. This would then run along the leading edge, the friction being such that it would cause a little smoke until it eventually whipped and wrapped itself around the wing. Only being attached to a parachute, the entire device was soon free of the aircraft but upon examination, it was found to have left a jagged cut in the leading edge. Imagine what damage a cable and balloon would have done. These early experiments contributed a great deal to the eventual deployment of the balloon barrage during the second conflict.

The new Balloon Command came into being on 1st November 1938. It was under the operational control of Fighter Command and the squadrons were manned mainly by men and women of the auxiliary air force, a total of 49 having been established by August 1940. A training unit had been set up at Cardington in Bedfordshire, the home of the ill-fated R.100 airships, on 9th January 1937 and by the first day of the war, Balloon Command had deployed a total of 444 balloons in London and about 180 elsewhere. Some were flown from permanent establishments and some were mobile, these being flown from winch-equipped lorries for versatile deployment. There was even a demand for water-borne balloons in order to counter the mine-laying enemy aircraft that flew over the estuaries. With all this demand, it was becoming increasingly difficult in the opening phases of the war for production to keep pace.

The people of London and the surrounding suburbs first saw the barrage around 5 pm on 3rd September 1939, the day war

20

broke out. A most extraordinary sight, the balloons were immediately christened 'Silver Giants' by the populus. Throughout the Battle of Britain and the years after, Balloon Command never faltered in their duty. Although after 1941 the enemy losses by colliding with balloons fell dramatically, the V1 campaign of 1944 saw the balloon come back into its own. As time went on, enemy pilots came to know the main areas to avoid but in the case of pilotless aircraft, the barrage did present a physical barrier.

It was early in December 1943 that news of Hitler's 'Revenge Weapon' came to the notice of the Air Ministry. Possibilities of defence measures were investigated with all speed including the use of the balloon barrage. It was further agreed to explore a proposal to form a 20 mile long protective curtain of guns, searchlights and balloons. The proposal was to site them to the south and south-east of London but as far as the balloons were concerned, they were to be sited on the high ground of the North

The defence of London and the surrounding counties was further entrusted to a series of forts built in the Thames Estuary. These remain to this day, though in a somewhat poor condition. (SE Newspapers)

Downs in order to take advantage of the extra height that the Downs gave.

One problem however was that by 1944 with fewer enemy aircraft flying over the country, the balloon personnel had been reduced accordingly, from 38,000 to 28,000. Additional requirements for D-Day+ had also to be taken into account but it was anticipated that around 500 balloons were needed. As the major threat appeared to be in the London area, the greater proportion would be placed in the south-east. Preparations went ahead with the completion of all the administrative arrangements, in place by February 1944. Balloon Command had set up two balloon centres, one at Biggin Hill and the other at Gravesend, both Battle of Britain airfields. However, the enemy threat to London did not materialise for four months, this time enabling the centres to carry out essential work at the sites in preparation, making central anchorages and cutting access and approach roads. Training in the handling of balloons was on-going so that by June, when the attacks began, everything was in place.

The defence against the 'Flying Bomb' was given the code name 'Diver'. By 1st July, 1,000 balloons had been deployed, twice the number originally envisaged, and up to 30th June, 53 bombs had impacted the cables. This result was encouraging and consideration was further given to deploying even more balloons in what was to become Phase II of Diver. However, before the completion of this phase, Phase III plans were drawn up for a further increase in balloons, up to 750 more.

June, July and early August were to see the brunt of the V1 attacks. By late August it was obvious that the rapid advances on the Continent together with the relentless bombing of the launch sites by the RAF had cancelled further launchings. From the deployment of the initial phase on 17th June 1944 to 4th September 1944, 1,937 V1s had entered the balloon belt. Of these, 407 had impacted the cables with 239 totally destroyed. On 8th September, Mr Duncan Sandys MP, the chairman of the Crossbow War Cabinet Committee (Crossbow being the code word for the attacks on the launch sites), gave a statement to the nation stating that but for the last few shots, the V1 campaign was over.

There is no doubt that the balloons were an effective defence yet some people today still question whether or not it was an effective use of resources. Hitler's next revenge weapon, the V2, could not be stopped by balloons, guns or aircraft. It dropped silently from space onto an unsuspecting public. It is, however, the sight of the 'Silver Giants' in the sky that most people remember.

Bentley Priory

Although the county of Middlesex only had three operational airfields during the Second World War, it did encompass the very impressive mansion known as Bentley Priory which became the headquarters of RAF Fighter Command. Situated near Stanmore, the building was designed and built for John James Hamilton, the 9th Earl and 1st Marquis of Abercorn. Upon his death the estate passed through various owners until 1883 when it came into the hands of Mr Frederick Gordon who intended turning it

The nerve centre of Fighter Command – the underground operations room at Stanmore in 1940. (IWM)

into a private hotel. With his death it became an exclusive girls' school which eventually lost money and was closed in 1924. Two years later and with no new owner in sight, the estate was divided and some 40 acres, including the mansion, was sold to the Air Ministry for the sum of around £25,000.

At around this time, the Air Defence of Great Britain and in particular, the Headquarters Inland Area, were proposing a move from nearby Uxbridge. They were given Bentley Priory and moved there on 26th May 1926. Ten years later and with the signs of another war apparent, the ADGB was split up into commands with Fighter Command taking effect from 14th July 1936, with Air Chief Marshal Dowding as its AOC-in-C. The building was again converted for its new role including the creation of an operations room and a filter room in two of the largest rooms.

As the prospect of war loomed ever closer, Bentley Priory began to take on a warlike appearance. Hedges and trees were cut down to give the impression of one enormous parkland, trenches and shelters were dug in the gardens and the building itself was heavily camouflaged. Later a large hole was to be excavated close to the Priory for the installation of the underground command centre.

Hugh Dowding was without doubt the architect of the system used to control the squadrons during the Battle of Britain. His ingenious method of reporting and control and his pushing for metal monoplanes instead of wooden biplanes, went a long way in helping to gain success in the air. A quiet man and known to many as 'Stuffy', his devotion to duty and his foresight would earn him the respect of the world, yet he was to be cruelly put out of office as the war progressed.

By July 1940, Fighter Command was divided into four groups, Nos 10, 11, 12 and 13 covering the south-west, south-east, central and northern parts of the country. The hole that had been excavated in the grounds of the Priory was now the nerve centre of the command. Over 58,000 tons of earth had been moved and over 17,000 tons of concrete had been poured into its construction. The system worked out by Dowding and his officers was that all information would be fed into the filter room. It would then be sorted and passed onto the adjoining operations room where in the form of coloured counters indicating the number of enemy aircraft approaching, it would be displayed on a large 'ops' table in the middle of the room as well as on maps around the walls. The counters would be changed and moved as conditions changed, usually by Waafs receiving information through their headsets. This mass of information would then be passed to the different groups and sector stations to operate and control the squadrons at the fighter airfields.

Information that came into Bentley Priory was from the Chain Home and Chain Home Low radar stations and the Observer Corps. In the case of the latter, information came via the Corps control centre, then to the Groups and Sectors before it got to Bentley Priory. Further information came from the 'Y' Service Wireless Listening Posts and also the Ultra decoding centre at Bletchley Park. All of this would be passed onto the headquarters of the various commands headed by officers of Air Vice-Marshal rank. In the case of No 10 Group it was AVM Sir Quintin Brand covering the south-west, for 11 Group it was AVM Keith Park covering the all important south-east, 12 Group had AVM Trafford Leigh-Mallory covering the Midlands and the Wash, and finally 13 Group with AVM Richard Saul covered the north. For closer control of the battle, each group was divided into sectors, each one controlling a number of airfields.

It was established from the beginning that Bentley Priory would take overall command of the static defences. Although commanded by Sir Frederick Pile, Anti-aircraft Command was also under the operational control of the Priory. It was also the headquarters of Balloon Command which in June 1940, had about 1,400 balloons on strength. With this prior knowledge of any raids that were about to materialise, Bentley Priory was also able to control the national Air Raid Warning System. For this they used colour codings to indicate various stages with a 'yellow' warning being issued when a raid was within 20 minutes flying time of a district. This would also warn local services, the Fire Service and the Police. If it was seen that a raid was making for a specific target, a 'red' warning would be issued. This would prompt the air raid sirens to sound. A 'green' colour would indicate that the raiders had passed and the sirens would then sound the 'all clear'.

Major General E.B. Ashmore, CB, CMG, MVO, instigator of the Royal Observer Corps, and (opposite) the Observer's book of rules – the 'bible' for ROC men and women. (D Wood)

FOR OFFICIAL USE ONLY.

This document is the property of H.B.M. Government.

NOTE.

The information given in this document is not to be communicated, either directly or indirectly, to the Press or to any other person not holding an official position in His Majesty's Service or in the **Observer Corps.**

AIR DEFENCE OF GREAT BRITAIN

INSTRUCTIONS

FOR

OBSERVER POSTS

1934.

By Command of the Air Council.

C. Ll. Bullock

THE AIR MINISTRY,

November, 1933.

It is sometimes questioned whether or not the German High Command knew of the existence of Bentley Priory for throughout the war, it never became a target for the Luftwaffe. The nearest incidents were when two small bombs landed close by and a V1 and V2 crashing some distance away broke some windows. It survived intact and continued its role as the headquarters of Fighter Command into peacetime. In 1968, Strike Command was formed and took over from the old Fighter and Bomber Commands, moving its headquarters to Uxbridge. The Priory became the headquarters of No 11 Group and even today, houses the Officers Mess for that group.

RAF Uxbridge

As with Bentley Priory, RAF Uxbridge comprised an historic house and land known as Hillingdon House. Built in 1717 for the Duke of Schomberg as a hunting lodge, it remained in private hands until acquired by the Government in 1915. It was rumoured that it was to be used for accommodating German POWs, but in the end it became a convalescent hospital for Canadian soldiers. It later became an Armament School which disbanded in June 1919. With the formation of the RAF from the RFC and the RNAS, the RAF School of Music arrived and Uxbridge also became the Recruits Training Depot.

Through the 1920s and the 1930s it continued in this vein but with the move to Bentley Priory of the Headquarters Inland Area in June 1926, the ADGB moved into Hillingdon House. In 1936, in a radical change due to the deteriorating situation in Germany, No 11 Group Fighter Command became established at Uxbridge together with the headquarters of Bomber Command. The Recruit Depot expanded with the increasing tension and a further reflection of the situation was seen when the excavation and building of an underground operations room was carried out in the south-east corner of the camp.

When war broke, it was this corner of Uxbridge from which AVM Keith Park controlled his squadrons in No 11 Group. Acting on information passed to him and his commanders from Bentley Priory, he directed his squadrons as the situation

*Air Chief Marshal Sir Keith Rodney Park, Commander of No 11 Group,
Fighter Command during the Battle of Britain. (IWM)*

dictated. The reporting set-up was similar to that of the Priory
with the controller and his assistants raised above the main
plotting table which was in the centre of the room. The squadrons
were represented by markers as were the enemy aircraft. The
Waaf plotters moved the markers as the scenario changed giving
an overall picture of the state of the battle. Park reported directly
to Dowding and like his boss, he was to be relieved of his
command directly after the Battle of Britain had been won. He
was posted to command a flying training group. Without these
two men, the battle may well have been lost.

Today, Uxbridge is the base for No 219 Communications
Squadron and is also the home of the Queen's Colour Squadron.
The operations room fell into disrepair for a few years but was
restored in 1975 to represent the 1940 period. It was officially
opened as a museum and although visits are only by prior
arrangement, it stands as a great reminder of Britain's darkest
hour and of the foresight of two great commanders.

Although some distance from the Thames Valley, the GIs on Romney Marsh helped to

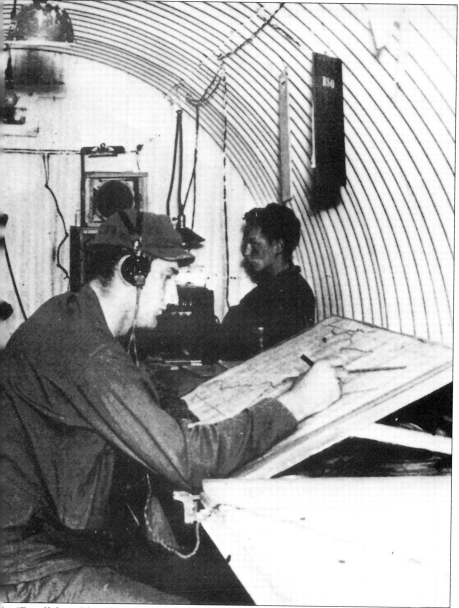

ie 'Doodlebugs' by plotting their height and range. (SE Newspapers)

Bletchley Park

Situated deep in the countryside of rural Buckinghamshire, five miles from Woburn Park, is a country house known as Bletchley Park. It is a large ornate family house of red brick and gables designed in the Victorian style. Comprising 20 or more rooms, the entire building is surrounded by spacious lawns. It had been requisitioned by the War Office before the war and was intended to be the evacuation headquarters of MI6. By the time war was declared, several huts had been erected in the grounds and it had acquired a name that was to become famous within the realms of intelligence. It was known as Station X.

Throughout the Second World War, the German High Command were sending signals to their commanders via a secret code known as Enigma. Though British Intelligence were able to intercept the signals, they were desperate to find a way to decode them. At Station X, work was already in progress to do just that.

The work began during 1938/9 when the Government Code and Cypher School was established at Bletchley Park. There was already a dedicated team using various methods of encyphering messages but somehow the Enigma system could not be broken. The only hope was for agents in Europe to attempt to find out what sort of cypher system the Germans were using but this would take time.

Meanwhile, in 1938, a Polish man employed in an eastern German factory suspected that the equipment that he was working on was a secret signalling machine. Being Polish and with his hate and distrust of the Germans, he made notes of the various parts of the machine and carefully concealed them in his home. With the war fast approaching and due to the fact that the Germans discovered his nationality, he was sacked and sent back to his own country, carefully managing to conceal and take his notes and sketches with him.

Once back home, he contacted a British agent in Warsaw who passed the information on to London. The man was smuggled into Paris where he was told to make a mock-up of the type of machinery that he had been working on. This he did and it was eventually passed to Bletchley Park where the experts were able to identify it as a mechanical cypher machine, called Enigma. What was now wanted was a complete, intact machine and it was here that the Polish Secret Service came to our aid. One Englishman, however, from Bletchley Park, Commander Alastair Denniston, did go to Poland to aid the Secret Service in their attempt which proved very successful. He brought back a new and complete electrically operated Enigma Cypher machine. Now all that was needed was to find the way in which the signals were decoded on the machine. This was to prove a very difficult task.

Enigma consisted of electrically connected revolving drums around which were placed the letters of the alphabet. A typewriter fed the letters of the message into the machine where they were so constructed into the signal by the revolving drums of the machine as to make them readable to anyone who knew the code. The scientists realised that it would take months to work out all the permutations for decoding the signal. It was indeed practically foolproof and the Germans knew it but work was already in hand at Station X, as it was now called, to break the code. This could only be done mathematically and so the station became the home for many brillant mathematicians.

It was at the end of February 1940 that the Luftwaffe had received enough Enigma machines and had trained enough operators to enable them to use the system on a very large scale, they being the first of the German commands to use Enigma. At Station X, the secret work had been given the code-name 'Ultra' and was already in the process of receiving all the signals being sent to the various Luftwaffe units.

Day after day, night after night, the scientists constantly struggled to break the code and thus give British intelligence the edge on the enemy. There was some information that could not be acted upon for that would have given the Germans the knowledge that we could decode their signals. Suffice to say, from the Battle of Britain to the assault upon mainland Europe, there is no doubt that Ultra helped the Allies to win the war. It gave them prior knowledge of the enemy's plans which allowed them to position their forces accordingly. Although Hitler and his top generals never gave any indication that England was able to break the code, they must surely have wondered why on earth their well laid plans were going wrong. It was General Eisenhower, the Supreme Allied Commander, who stated that Ultra was decisive in the outcome of the war. Without it, history may well have been very different.

Today, Station X is a museum showing much of what went on during the war, though some parts are still subject to the Official Secrets Act. Sadly, in March 2000, the Enigma decoding machine on display was stolen.

The USAAF and Music

Wherever there were American servicemen and women, there was music. Service in the UK was no exception with bands such as Sam Donahue's Navy Band making regular appearances and broadcasts after they arrived in April 1944. Yet despite the appeal of his band and several others, one outfit stood out from all of them, that of Glenn Miller.

Still a major talking point today regarding his mysterious disappearance, Glenn had led a successful civilian band for five years before he disbanded it and joined the Army Air Force. As Captain and later Major, Glenn formed the American Band of the Allied Expeditionary Force (AEF) which played at many of the major venues in the UK. Prior to their arrival over here, on 29th May 1943, the orchestra broadcast the first of six test programmes over the CBS network titled *I Sustain the Wings*. With their signature tune, *Moonlight Serenade*, they were an outstanding success and continued for nearly a year.

It was however, during the planning for D-Day that it was suggested that an American dance band be sent to London to broadcast, to the Allied forces once they had established a hold on Europe. Glenn was approached on the strength of his successful broadcasts, to which he said an emphatic 'yes' and the orchestra, comprising some 60 members, embarked on the *Queen Elizabeth* and sailed for Scotland.

They arrived at Gourock on 28th June 1944, disembarked and travelled to London to meet up with Glenn and his radio producer, Sergeant Paul Dudley. On the evening of Sunday 9th July, Glenn Miller and the band of the AEF made their first

Glenn Miller pictured when he fronted his civilian orchestra during 1941.
(The Gramophone Company)

broadcast over the American Forces Network and the BBC Home
Service. There then began a gruelling schedule of concerts, some
of which included the Thames Valley airfields and operational
headquarters, and are listed below.

25th July 1944 – Greenham Common Airfield – Station 486. The

35

THAMES VALLEY AIRFIELDS IN THE SECOND WORLD WAR

The American Band of the AEF led by Glenn Miller give a concert at Wycombe Abbey on 29th July 1944. The clarinet player is the legendary 'Peanuts' Hucko. (Plaistow Pictorial)

band were picked up from Twinwoods Farm airfield in three C-47s of the 438th TCG; the aircraft were named *Skylark, Patches* and *Patsy Ann*. They gave a two hour concert in a marquee erected for the occasion. In the evening they gave a concert in the Newbury Corn Exchange.

29th July 1944 – Wycombe Abbey – Station 101. Command headquarters of the US 8th Air Force.

16th August 1944 – Bentley Priory. A special concert was performed in the afternoon on the lawn behind the Officers' Mess. Whilst the band were playing, a V1 rocket appeared overhead. Glenn conducted the band to play quietly so as to hear the pulse rocket engine lest it stopped overhead.

16th August 1944 – Though not on the concert list, RAF Hendon was the scene of a near accident involving Glenn's aircraft. As they were about to land, a red flare shot up from the tower and they aborted the landing. The reason was that a B-17 was taking off at the same time as they were landing.

The disappearance of Glenn Miller is well documented. Several theories have been put forward, the most plausible being the fact that his Norseman plane entered a bomb dumping area just off the Sussex coast when Lancaster bombers high overhead were dumping their bombs from an aborted operation. It is recorded from a navigator of one of the Lancasters, Fred Shaw, that he noticed a small aircraft below crossing the dumping area.

Despite this explanation and several highly unlikely others, no definitive answer has ever been found and the mystery lingers on as well as the music. There is no doubt that the morale of all servicemen and women was lifted by his music and today, *Moonlight Serenade* is as popular as ever. In the UK alone there are four bands consistently in demand to give concerts of Miller's music. In no particular order of excellence, there are the Syd Lawrence Band, the Herb Miller Orchestra led by Glenn's nephew, John, the Glenn Miller UK Orchestra and just recently, the Ray McVay Band. Each and every one of them keeps the music and the nostalgia of the period alive.

2

ALDERMASTON

One of the targets during the 1950s for 'Ban the Bomb' protestors was Aldermaston airfield, a few miles south-east of Aldermaston village in Berkshire. With its closure by the Ministry of Civil Aviation in 1950, it became the Atomic Weapons Research Establishment, a post that is continued today. Before this however, it was a major troop-carrying airfield.

As with many airfields in the area, Aldermaston was built and developed as a bomber OTU in 1941. Ready by 1st July 1942, it became part of No 92 Group but was not used in its intended role. Instead it was allocated to the USAAF. The arrival of the 60th Troop Carrier Group comprising the 10th, 11th, 12th and 28th Troop Carrier Squadrons was completed by September 1942 and Aldermaston became Airfield No 467 on 20th October.

C-47s soon began to arrive but with the opening of the second front in North Africa, the 60th were transferred to the 12th Air Force. Operation Torch began in October 1942 and on 6th November, the C-47s left for Portreath in Cornwall before going overseas. By this time, four 'T' Type hangars had been constructed on the main airfield and in the vicinity of one of the dispersal areas another shed had been built. This was taken over by Vickers in July 1943 for Spitfire assembly and when complete, the aircraft were test flown from Aldermaston. This assembly plant was to continue until the end of the war was in sight.

With the departure of the Americans, Aldermaston returned very briefly to RAF control. A detachment of No 3 GTS arrived in late 1942, eventually turning out to be the only RAF unit to ever use the base. They stayed for a brief period before the next American unit eventually arrived. The 315th TCG came in on 12th December 1942 with their C-47s and C-53s arriving in February 1943. Consisting of the 34th and 43rd TCS, they soon received their own gliders in the form of Waco CG-4A Hadrians.

Unlike British gliders which were of wooden construction, the Hadrian was of mixed construction with a steel tubular fuselage. It carried a crew of two and could accommodate 13 troops, far less than the British gliders. Apart from Sicily, Hadrians were not used by the RAF, but they were one of the standard gliders used by the USAAF.

With the gliders arriving in May, the 315th sent some on detachment to assist in the Sicilian landings. During their absence, the group was transferred to the 9th Air Force and moved over to Welford in November 1943.

Aldermaston now became the home of the 370th Fighter Group and the 71st Fighter Wing headquarters. The 370th had become one of the three Lightning-equipped fighter units of the 9th Air Force. With its distinctive twin boom tail, the Lockheed Lightning performed a wide variety of missions in every war theatre and was to eventually destroy more Japanese aircraft in the Pacific than any other fighter. It was also intended to use the type in RAF service but after taking a delivery of three, they rejected the type and subsequently cancelled an order for 524 Mk.IIs. These were taken over by the USAAF, some of which eventually found their way to Aldermaston.

Yet again the stay was shortlived and it was not until 3rd March 1944 that Aldermaston really came into its own. By then the 9th Air Force Air Support Command headquarters had exchanged names with the 19th ASC. Personnel and equipment stayed the same, just the name changed. This allowed the 434th TCG to arrive from Fulbeck. The four squadrons, 71st, 72nd, 73rd and 74th immediately began intense training with their complement of C-47s. This was carried out in conjunction with the 101st Airborne Division, the intensity increasing as D-Day approached.

A Jeep towing a troop-carrying glider to the runway, where it will be hitched to a C-4 6 men, or one 37 mm anti-tank gun and crew, while the towing ship carried 18 airbor

May 1943, 315th Troop Carrier Group. The glider could carry 16 men, or one jeep and (Signal Corps)

As the men and women prepared for the great day, a vast cloak of security was thrown around the airfield. A BBC commentator at the time captured this tense atmosphere:

'This base and many more like it are sealed because we have been told the answers. The answers to the questions that the whole world had been asking for two years or more. Where and how and when! Troops swarmed around last night, strong, healthy, formidable men. Many of them going into battle for the first time.'

At dawn on 6th June, the C-47s towed 52 Hadrians carrying men of the 81st Airborne AA Battalion. Once again, the BBC were there to record the historic moment:

Ready for D-Day Plus 1, the Waco Hadrian gliders are lined up at Aldermaston awaiting the troops of the Carrier Group. (After the Battle)

Lieutenant General Brereton, Commander 1st Allied Airborne Army, talking at Aldermaston to Colonel Whiteacre, CO of 434th Troop Carrier Group, and Colonel Joseph Harper of 327th Glider Infantry Regiment of 101st Airborne Division. This is 18th September 1944 – the second day of Operation Market Garden. (National Archives via After the Battle)

'The first aircraft that is going to lead in the early hours of tomorrow morning is turning at the end of the tarmac to make its take-off. A graceful machine, its wingtip lights shining red and green over the heads of the smaller figures of people on the aerodrome watching it take off. Taking off from here, loaded with parachutists and taking with it perhaps the hopes and the fears of millions of people in this country who sleep tonight, not knowing that this mighty operation is taking place. There she goes now, the first aircraft leaving. Faster and faster and up into the air as we wave far below and wish them God speed and good luck.'

It was still moonlight when the first C-47 crossed the coast. Encountering a lot of flak, several aircraft were caught by

43

accurate gun-fire but 49 aircraft reached the drop zone and released their gliders. Several failed to make the exact landing site and landed among trees a mile inland from the Omaha Beach. This area was infested with enemy artillery and many good men who landed by air and sea never returned. The losses were high, but eventually a bridgehead was established.

For days after the initial assault, the group continued to drop supplies as well as training for the next big operation, Arnhem. On 17th September for Operation Market Garden, the 434th TCG carried the 82nd Airborne Division to Nijmegen followed by further supply drops. This continued into 1945 when they flew to a new base on mainland Europe at Mourmelon-le-Grand on 12th February.

With victory finally in sight, the 9th Air Force handed Aldermaston back to the RAF. A branch of Technical Training Command arrived, together with No 25 (RCAF) Aircrew Holding Unit for the purpose of recruiting men to continue the fight against Japan. Disbanding in December 1945, Aldermaston entered a period of Care and Maintenance which was to continue until 9th May 1946 when BOAC arrived and the airfield was given over to civil aviation. Dakotas, Oxfords and Yorks now used the facilities, later joined by such large aircraft as the Halifax. On 1st January 1947, Airways Training Ltd formed a school on the site, but by November 1948 this had closed and the number of movements from Aldermaston began to dwindle. For a short period, Eagle Aviation were based there but when the airfield was relinquished by the Ministry of Civil Aviation in April 1950, the Atomic Weapons Research Establishment moved in.

When the nuclear strikes on Hiroshima and Nagasaki had brought Japanese resistance to an end in 1946, a new type of warfare had been unleashed, one that was to threaten the very existence of mankind. The shape of the Cold War had been confirmed in 1949 and Britain, along with America, was about to enter the nuclear age. Resources were put into a programme to develop the weapons of mass destruction by scientists such as Professors Penney, Hinton and Cockcroft. An atomic bomb was first tested and exploded in 1952 on the Monte Bello Islands in Australia. This prompted an organisation calling themselves the Campaign for Nuclear Disarmament to hold rallies all over the

Post-war Aldermaston showing the large wartime hangars. It had changed little since 1944. (Aeroplane via F. Cheeseman)

The ultimate result of the work at Aldermaston post-war. The explosion of the British atomic bomb at Monte Belloe Island, Australia. (Crown copyright)

country. 'Ban the Bomb' became the fashionable slogan of the day and Aldermaston one of their principal targets.

Aldermaston today is a very sensitive site and should not be approached in any way. Many of the wartime buildings have gone and have given way to a housing estate on the south of the airfield. Though the Cold War has warmed up, research development into weapons of mass destruction still continues at Aldermaston.

3

CHEDDINGTON

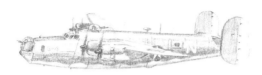

During the war, many famous construction companies were involved in the task of building airfields. McAlpine, Laing and Mowlem were among them, with one of the foremost being George Wimpey and Co Ltd. Once the acquisition of farming land from irate landowners, farmers and local authorities had been completed under the Emergency Powers (Defence) Act of 1939, the large construction companies moved in to demolish obstructions and begin the process of making the ground suitable for aircraft. This scenario was repeated in most cases and was certainly the case for George Wimpey when given the contract to build Cheddington.

Situated in a low-lying area 30 miles north-west of London and bordering the county of Hertfordshire, the Buckinghamshire village of Cheddington was set in a triangle completed by the villages of Long Marston and Ivinghoe. It first came to the attention of the 'Aerodrome Board' during 1940 but it did not come into use until 1942. The land requisitioned had been farmed for many years and although the official from the 'Board' had inspected the area during 1940, the farmers did not believe that the site would be appropriate. Imagine their surprise and dismay when, during early 1941, they were told that their land had been requisitioned in order that an airfield could be built.

A local contractor, B. Sunley Ltd, was given the initial task of

The notorious 'Southend Hill' at the intersection of one of the Cheddington runways. It was this natural hill that made landings and take-offs so difficult.

clearing the site. Progress, however, was too slow for the ministry and a contract was awarded to George Wimpey to take over the momentous task. They had soon finished the earth moving work and continued to cut and lay out the runways together with the erection of the necessary buildings. The final construction was the control tower that was designed to a Type 13079/41 layout. With all the building work complete, the site was handed over to the military.

The airfield was allocated to the RAF and was deemed to be a bomber training airfield. It initially became the headquarters of No 26 Operational Training Unit when the nearby airfield of Wing, originally allocated for the OTU, was not completed in time. On 15th March 1942, the men of the OTU Servicing Squadron arrived to be followed by four Avro Ansons on 22nd March. The next day the first of the Vickers Wellingtons arrived, and by the end of the month the strength stood at 17 Wellingtons and 6 Ansons.

By bomber airfield standards, Cheddington was quite small

and not really ideal for training pilots. The longest runway was 1,780 yards long and the obstructions and hills surrounding the airfield made approach and departure very interesting! So much so that at one time during its use as an RAF station, reports were submitted that Cheddington was unfit for military training purposes. As if to emphasise the point, several fatal accidents involving the Wellingtons occurred at the airfield.

The first aircraft loss was on 31st May, in this instance not due to the airfield but to enemy action. Wellington EU-D, serial no DV707, was reported missing after the '1,000 bomber raid' on Cologne. Three others were 'struck off charge' during August due to incidents at Cheddington, but one of the worst tragedies occurred on 30th August 1942. Wellington EU-U, serial no DV825, was taking off for a training session of circuits and landings when it suddenly lost speed. Struggling to control the aircraft, the pilot, Sergeant McDougall, swung it round and stalled whilst trying to clear the hill to the south of Cheddington. With a 'crump', the aircraft came down and burst into flames. Despite being pulled clear of the aircraft by two local farmers, Sergeant McDougall and one of the gunners, Sergeant Hendrickson, sadly lost their lives. For their heroic efforts, Gordon Miller and Dan Millis were awarded the British Empire Medal.

By the end of August 1942, Wing had become operational and, as was originally intended, No 26 OTU moved their operation to the newly opened airfield. For a month Cheddington was without aircraft, until 7th September when it was handed over to the United States 8th Army Air Force.

Events taking place in Europe and the perceived threat of the Japanese in south-east Asia and the Pacific had finally led President Roosevelt to request on 12th January 1939, that the American Air Corps be expanded. By 1941, Army regulation 95-5 had created the Army Air Force, this being a combined force of the Air Corps and the GHQ Air Force under the authority of Major General H.H. Arnold. At the same time as this combination and expansion was taking place, the Roosevelt government negotiated a 99 year lease with His Majesty's Government on military bases to be located throughout the various countries with allegiance to the British Empire. The Army Air Forces of America were about to arrive in Europe.

By December 1941, the USAAF had 71 operational groups: 27 Bombardment, 24 Pursuit, 11 Observation, 6 Transport, 2 Composite and 1 Photographic. On 22nd December 1941, three weeks after the United States had been forced into war by the Japanese at Pearl Harbor, Mr Churchill arrived in Washington for talks with President Roosevelt. During talks and discussions, the two men and their Chiefs-of-Staff agreed that the war effort against Germany was to take priority over the Japanese as soon as the Japanese advances could be halted. Part of the plan was that the Americans would establish an Army Air Force in Britain to mount bombing operations against Germany and occupied Europe. This force was to be known as the 8th Air Force, which became operational in April 1942 and would primarily include Bombardment (Heavy) and Fighter Groups as well as some Bombardment (Medium), Reconnaissance and Troop Carrier Groups with Support Units. It was one of the heavy bombardment groups, the 44th Bomb Group, that was allocated to Cheddington.

With the ground echelon leaving America aboard the *Queen Mary*, the journey to England began. Arriving in Scotland five days later, the men disembarked and joined trains to take them to Cheddington. Back in America, the B-24D Liberators prepared to fly across the Atlantic. This they successfully did, arriving at their new base on 1st October 1942. Nine Liberators of the 66th Squadron touched down to cheers and clapping from the already arrived groundcrews. A look at the base and its surrounding hills, plus the difficulty that some of the aircraft had found in approaching Cheddington, did not exactly endear the airfield to them. The Americans, however, found comfort in tasting English beer and acquainting themselves with the English way of life.

Their fears of flying from Cheddington were short-lived for it had already been realised that the Liberator was far too large and too heavy to fly from this small airfield. Accordingly, on 30th October, the 44th moved over to Shipdham in Norfolk. It had however been readily accepted by all the 8th Air Force commanders in England that American crews would have to undergo training in British military procedures. For General Eaker, the commander general of the US 8th Air Force, this became a

50

A B-24 Liberator receives a direct hit whilst on a raid to Hamburg. Its crew were possibly trained at one of the USAAF bases in the Thames Valley. (US Air Force)

priority issue and he requested Washington to form a number of Combat Crew Replacement Centres at various UK bases. When the 44th, nicknamed 'The Flying Eightballs', left for Shipdham, Cheddington became the 12th Combat Crew Replacement Centre which specialised in the training of B-24 Liberator crews.

Cheddington was now to undergo a period of expansion. During the next four months the runway was resurfaced and the living, technical and recreation sites were enlarged. The lie of the land around the airfield did not, however, allow the runways and landing areas to be extended, a fact that was to restrict the use of Cheddington for its entire existence. Work had been completed by January 1943, allowing the airfield to return briefly to RAF use. No 2 Gliding School arrived to take part in an exercise. With a complement of Hotspur gliders and Miles Master Mk.II tugs, 1,182 day and 287 night tows had been accomplished before the unit moved to Weston-on-the-Green, leaving Cheddington once again vacant.

Across the Atlantic, a new bomber wing had been formed. Attached at the beginning to the 3rd Air Force, it was soon to be reassigned to the 8th. The wing underwent a period of intense training before it left for Camp Shanks in New York on 8th May 1943 prior to an overseas posting. Though the men in the unit did not know the final destination nor the name of their new unit, Headquarters Army Air Corps did. The base was to be Cheddington and the unit was titled the 20th Bomb Wing (Heavy). Its duty was to be in support of the daylight bombing of Germany.

The new arrivals spent the first few weeks in the 8th Bomber Command Headquarters at High Wycombe before moving to Cheddington. In the meantime, the *Queen Mary* had once again crossed the 'pond' carrying further men and machines. These were from the 379th Service Squadron, 9th Station Complement

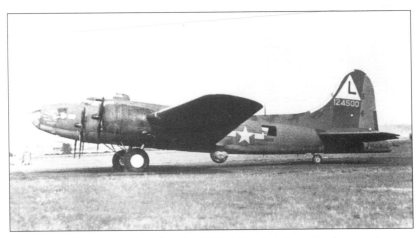

The first real bomber assigned to the 2901st Combat Crew Replacement Group at Cheddington was a war-weary B-17E Fortress, seen here at dispersal. (R. Burri, 113 Association)

Squadron mechanics at Cheddington receive training on a B-17 oxygen system with the help of the B-17 mobile training wagon and a B-17 called 'Flak Alley Lil'.

Squadron, 1077th Signal Company and the 39th Service Group. These were all bound for Cheddington, making it for the first time in its existence, a combat-ready base.

Several specialist units were now able to use the new facilities. One of these was the 'Night Leaflet Squadron', the 858th Bomb Squadron. It was after the Allied invasion in June 1944 that this type of psychological warfare really came into its own. The idea of the campaign was that leaflets would be dropped over enemy-occupied territory declaring that, with the rapid progress of the Allies towards Germany, it would be futile for the enemy to continue to offer up resistance. For them, they were told, the war was nearly over. The other section to be targeted from leaflet drops were the foreign workers, who were encouraged to do all they could to sabotage the German war machine. As if to emphasise the importance that leaflet drops held for the war effort, in June 1944 the 858th dropped 209.6 tons; in July, out of 133 sorties, 216.1 tons were dropped; whilst August saw an even larger increase in sorties and tons delivered. With this increasing pressure, seven new crews arrived from the 856th Bomb Squadron, 492nd Bomb Group, these being further supplemented by five crews from the 36th Bomb Group. They came

53

with B-24 Liberators, as Major Earle J. Aber succeeded Colonel Hambaugh as the CO. The 858th Bomb Group passed into history, as the title of the enlarged unit was changed to the 496th Bomb Squadron (Night Leaflet).

A very hectic period of drops began with further crews arriving to assist. With night operations, obviously the weather was of the utmost importance. Immediate and accurate weather forecasting was essential and in order that the Cheddington crews got just this, a detachment of the 18th Weather Squadron arrived at the airfield. Situated in a separate room in the control tower, their duty was to see that every crew on operations were given a set of maps showing fronts, pressure centres, precipitation areas, cloud base top and bottom and the expected take-off and landing conditions. Further charts showed wind speeds (essential when dropping leaflets), areas of suspected icing and of course, structural hazards that were apparent if the crews flew at low level. Despite all this information, there were bound to be fatalities.

Leaflets being packed into Monroe bombs by the ammunition company based in Bedfordshire. They were later transported to Cheddington. (IWM)

There is only room to mention but two incidents in this chapter, one of which turned out right and one that did not. There were many others, some as bad, some worse and some just minor. With a squadron combination of the B-17 Fortress and the B-24 Liberator, there is no common denominator for such tragedies. Perhaps their luck just ran out.

On 16th August 1944, B-17 42-30791 left Cheddington on a night leaflet mission. Intending to cover five targets, it was whilst over the third that an engine fire in No 1 engine caused a problem for its pilot, Lieutenant D. Bailey and his crew. Feathering the engine, he put the B-17 into a dive and levelled off at 23,000 feet. Though the fire was put out, the engine was out of action and thus, the speed of the aircraft was affected. Letting down to 15,000 feet, they were attacked by an enemy aircraft. Taking evasive action with all the guns blazing at the enemy, Lieutenant Bailey threw his aircraft, named *Pistol Packin' Mama*, into a series of turns. The accuracy of the gunners caused the enemy aircraft to blow up in front of the Fortress with pieces of it hitting the fuselage of the bomber. Despite the problem, the B-17 managed to get home safely and was credited with one kill.

A Boeing B-17 on a raid over Germany.

55

The US Army WAACs arrive at Cheddington in 1944. Mainly employed on admin duties, they proved a great asset to the US Army. (M. Hunt, 113 Association)

Not so lucky, however, were Lieutenant Chester Cherrington and his crew. Flying a B-24 Liberator on a cross country flight, their aircraft was lost when it collided with a chimney at Burghill Mental Hospital near Hereford whilst, for some unknown reason, flying at only 100 feet. Crashing in flames, the crew of ten were killed outright. It was incidents like this that brought back the feeling that 'death was just around the corner'.

In September, a total of 105 aircraft were sent out to dispatch 1,050 leaflet bombs to 313 targets. October and November were the same and as 1944 came to a very cold ending, it was the culmination of a very successful period at Cheddington.

The NLS were not, however, the only specialist unit on the base. In August 1944, the 803rd Bomb Squadron had merged with the 856th Bomb Squadron and was now known as the 36th Bomb Squadron (H) (RCM). A Radio Countermeasures Squadron, they moved to Cheddington later the same month and shared the operations room with the NLS.

A Radio Countermeasures B-24 Liberator 'Beast of Bourbon' taxies at Cheddington in 1945. (R Freeman)

Similar operations continued for the rest of the year and into 1945. With victory in Europe, Cheddington was returned to RAF Bomber Command on 21st June where it became a base in No 26 Group. It remained in this capacity for a year until on 1st May 1946, the airfield transferred to the Technical Training Command and was occupied by the Medical Training Establishment. Renamed RAF Marsworth on 13th August 1946, the medical unit remained until 16th February 1948 when the station was declared surplus to requirements and was closed. It quickly fell into disrepair but later part of the site became a sub-depot of the Central Ordnance.

In 1977 the final closure of the camp took place, with part of it being retained by the Department of the Environment. Cheddington was not the airmen's favourite airfield, but it served its purpose adequately during a period of intense pressure.

4

GREENHAM COMMON

Intended for use as a bomber Operational Training Unit like so many other sites in Berkshire, Greenham Common was eventually to become a USAAF base. Lying on a ridge between the Kennet and Enborne rivers, construction started early in 1942. It was to be one of the larger airfields with a main runway 4,800 feet in length and two secondary runways, one being 4,050 feet and the other 3,300 feet. Several minor roads crossing the ridge had to be closed to accommodate the site with the main Newbury-Basingstoke road being allowed to remain open, but fitted with barriers for closing when aircraft were operational. Even then, the airfield was found not to be large enough and a period of further enlargement took place during late 1942. The accommodation area was constructed around the eastern perimeter with two T2 hangars being erected together with a technical site and a 27-pan hardstanding perimeter area.

Though the airfield was not completely finished, the headquarters staff of the 51st Troop Carrier Wing arrived from the USA in September 1942. With Operation Torch, the invasion of French North Africa taking place in October, the 51st TCW moved to North Africa the following month. Responsibility for Greenham Common was transferred back to the RAF and No 70 Group. The arrival of No 15 Air Firing Unit and No 1511 Beam Approach Training Flight on 28th April 1943 brought the

Airspeed Oxford to Greenham. The RAF's first twin-engined monoplane advanced trainer, it became the workhorse of the force, being used in a wide variety of essential roles.

For five months they were the only aircraft stationed at Greenham but when the airfield was again required by the Americans, they were forced to move elsewhere. An area adjacent to the main airfield known as Crookham Common was also requisitioned as an assembly plant for the Waco gliders that were arriving in crates from the USA. Once assembled, they were towed by road onto the airfield proper before being taken to other airfields. As the plans for the invasion of Europe developed, assembly increased from 15 to 50 a day just prior to 'Overlord'.

On 1st October 1943, Greenham Common became USAAF Station 486 and was handed over to the 9th Air Force for the use of, not troop aircraft, but fighters. Duly, the personnel of the 354th Fighter Group arrived to find that they were to be given the new P-51D Mustang. One of the most outstanding fighter aircraft of the war, its performance was superior to any other American fighter and it was one of the few American fighters to be used by

American troops relax at one of the American bases. (SE Newspapers)

the RAF. The aircraft used by the 354th were powered by the British Rolls-Royce Merlin engine, this proving superior to the earlier American Allison engine. As a fighter, the Mustang was to escort the large American bomber formations that were to bomb Germany by day, in the process becoming known as the 'Little Friends'. The 354th, the 'Pioneer Mustang Group', worked up on the type for a week before moving to Boxted in Essex.

They were replaced by the HQ of the 70th Fighter Wing, who were in turn replaced by the 100th Fighter Wing on 6th December 1943. In a period of rapid change, the new year saw the 368th Fighter Group arrive bringing the first Republic P-47 Thunderbolts to fly from Greenham Common. Affectionately known as 'the Jug', the aircraft was first introduced to the European Theatre of Operations on 10th March 1943. The size and weight of the aircraft dismayed the pilots of the USAAF, but the addition of drop tanks and an increased size of internal tanks turned it into a suitable long-range, high altitude aircraft. Yet again, they only stayed to briefly work up on the P-47 before moving on to Chilbolton in Hampshire (see *Hampshire Airfields in the Second World War*). They did, however, carry out one mission from Greenham, that of flying to the French coast on 14th March 1944. No combat took place and all 48 aircraft of the group returned safely to base.

A reorganisation of the command dictated that Greenham Common was to become a Troop Carrier base. Accordingly, no further fighters were to be stationed there as it became the home of the 438th TCG on 16th March 1944. The four squadrons incorporated in the 438th were the 87th, 88th, 89th and the 90th, all flying the familiar C-47 or C-53. As with all the other troop carrier bases, there began a period of intense glider training. Considerable changes had to be made to the airfield to allow for mass stream take-offs, the quickest way to get such great formations of aircraft airborne. The 438th were earmarked to lead the airborne forces to the dropping zones on 5th/6th June and consequently, the eve of the invasion saw a string of top military personnel at the base, including the Supreme Commander, General Dwight Eisenhower.

At 10.45 pm on 5th June 1944, 81 aircraft and their gliders took off from Greenham Common carrying the men of the 101st

Troops of the 101st Airborne Division seated in their glider ready for take-off at Greenham Common during D-Day rehearsals. (War Dept, Washington)

Airborne Division. The Channel crossing was uneventful and the gliders were cast off soon after midnight in the area of Carentan. Returning to Greenham Common, the C-47s were later tasked with towing Hadrian and Horsa gliders containing the troop reinforcements. Sadly, a C-47 and a C-53 were lost to heavy flak but for this and other work, the Group received a Distinguished Unit Citation.

With 'Overlord' a success, three squadrons of the 438th – the 87th, 88th and 89th – were deployed to Canino in Italy to take part in the invasion of Southern France. The 90th Squadron moved over to Welford for the duration, all the units returning to Greenham on 24th August 1944.

It was Operation Market Garden that the 438th were next tasked with. In common with all the other troop-carrying bases in the area, 90 aircraft dropped paratroops of the 101st Airborne Division near Eindhoven on 17th September. For the next two

An insulated container of blood is made ready for despatch in a Dakota to the battlefields of Normandy on 14th June 1944 at Greenham Common. (War Dept, Washington)

days, further glider missions were flown, the 19th being a day of several losses. With 40 aircraft towing gliders and leaving Greenham Common in difficult weather, one C-47 was hit by flak and lost whilst several gliders cast off too early and were also lost. The next few days were given over to dropping supplies to the troops below, with a glider-towing mission on 23rd September being the last for the 438th. With the rapid advances in Europe, they moved to Prosnes in France in February 1945.

The assembly of the Waco gliders continued for a time, the final number being over 4,000. This ceased with the ending of the war and Greenham Common was handed back to the RAF and Transport Command. In August a transfer to Technical Training Command brought to the base the sound of raw recruits being given drill instruction, perhaps an ignominious end for such a

A critical cargo of whole blood is rushed to a waiting plane. (National Archives)

large transport airfield. On 1st June 1946, Greenham Common was declared surplus to requirements and quickly fell into disrepair.

It would have continued this way but for a sudden escalation in the tensions between East and West. The Cold War of the 1950s saw a resurgence in use of the airfield and with it firmly back in the hands of the United States Air Force, large extensions were built to the runway and technical areas. Underground bunkers were built to house nuclear missiles, for a new and sinister type of warfare had arrived. USAF jet bombers and later Cruise missiles were to be deployed to Greenham, this bringing the wrath of the CND and the local people.

During the late 1970s and the early 1980s, it was the scene of many anti-nuclear demonstrations, which resulted in the setting up of a 'Women's Peace Camp' around the perimeter of the airfield. This grew to enormous proportions with the arrival of the Cruise missiles, which attracted extensive press and media coverage. Attempts to break in at Greenham Common usually resulted in arrests but not even this action could deter the women and their supporters.

Today, this is no more and much of the airfield has been sold to developers. Thirty three glider crews were killed flying from Greenham and are remembered every year on 12th December when a service is held in their memory. There still remains a small 'peace camp' around the perimeter, just in case the Cold War should revive. With so many internal wars in Europe and beyond, who can say what may happen?

5
HENDON

The order of battle for the RAF in January 1939 stated that Hendon, under the command of Wing Commander V. Buxton, had no fewer than four resident squadrons – No 24 (Commonwealth), 600 (City of London), 601 (County of London) and 604 (County of Middlesex), the last three being auxiliaries. It was a station within No 11 Group yet despite its position near London, in the county of Middlesex, it was not officially classified as a fighter station. It became known more as a communications base and in this respect, No 24 (Commonwealth) Squadron was the longest serving squadron at any airfield in the UK. They arrived on 9th July 1933 and remained at Hendon until 25th February 1946. Now the home of the RAF Museum, Hendon's history lies in dusty files and the memories of the people who served there.

The erection of a shed in a corner of a meadow was the first sign of aviation at Hendon. It was built to house a monoplane built by Messrs Everett and Edgecombe which sadly never left the ground. It fell to a young man by the name of Claude Grahame-White to first fly from the field. He gained his pilot's licence on 4th January 1910 and was the first Englishman to be issued with a certificate from the French Aero Club. He brought a Farman biplane to England and first tested it flying from

Hendon. By 1910 he had become involved with a company interested in developing Hendon as the London Aerodrome. He later started a flying school of his own and with the help of the Dunlop Company, purchased the site outright, expanding the flying area at the same time.

Grahame-White turned Hendon into a mecca for the rich and famous. He put on flying displays, the likes of which had never been seen before. He organised air rallies, as well as offering flying lessons to anyone who could afford it. He started the first Air Mail service between Hendon and Windsor which was hailed a great success. All of this, however, came to an end in 1914 when, with the First World War, Grahame-White's aircraft and facilities were requisitioned by the military and Hendon became a Royal Naval Air Station.

Pilots still continued to learn to fly with his company although the airfield also became No 2 Aircraft Acceptance Park for new aircraft. The RNAS set up a Defence Flight for London at the same time that the Royal Flying Corps began using Hendon. Aircraft manufacture continued eventually with the Grahame-White works on Aerodrome Road, Airco (De Havilland) on the Edgware Road and Handley Page just down the road at Kingsbury. The field was further used for experimental aircraft testing but with the armistice in 1918, an abrupt halt came to Hendon's military use.

Despite this, it remained under military ownership, much to the consternation of Grahame-White. With the cessation of hostilities, aircraft manufacture stopped overnight and White was forced to turn his works over to cars and furniture making. He finally ceased business in 1920 after many years at Hendon. The airfield was about to enter a new era.

With ownership still with the military, the RAF began a series of highly acclaimed Tournaments. Throughout the 1920s and 1930s, Hendon attracted thousands of people to its lush grass. Taking over the complete ownership in 1925, the RAF now used it for training the auxiliary squadrons and by 1927, several had become resident. No 600 (City of London) Squadron had formed at Northolt as a light bomber unit on 14th October 1925. It moved to Hendon on 18th January 1927 equipped with the De Havilland 9A, a single seat biplane which could carry a 450 lb bomb. A few

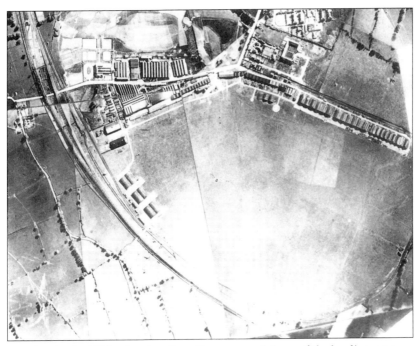

*Hendon in the 1920s showing the rather unusual shape of the landing area.
(PHT Green)*

days later they were joined by No 601 (County of London), also equipped with the DH9A. A friendly rivalry sprang up between these two auxiliary squadrons for as much as both squadrons were formed at the same time, 600 were to recruit people from all walks of life and were commanded by the Right Honourable Edward Guest whilst 601 recruited the rich and exclusive and became known as the 'millionaires mob'. They had been hand chosen by Lord Edward Grosvenor. This 'upper crust' dominance was further strengthened in 1930 when the Royal aircraft of Prince Edward, Prince of Wales and his brother, Prince Albert, arrived. They flew the Airspeed Envoy, the flight at one time having four of the type on strength.

By 1929, both auxiliary units had converted to the Westland Wapiti and were thrilling the Hendon crowds with their daring displays of air drill and fake bombing attacks. 1937 saw a change

The Westland Wapitis of No 604 Auxiliary Squadron in front of the squadron hangar at Hendon. They later moved to Northolt. (MAP)

to the Hawker Hart, this in turn followed by the Hawker Demon. This was a fighter variant of the Hart but was still a biplane. The monoplanes were still some time in the future. No 604 Squadron followed a similar pattern of aircraft when they moved through the Wapiti, Hart and Demon until they received the Blenheim I on 9th January 1939. This was the day fighter variant and was a development of the Type 142. So impressed with this aircraft were the military that it was ordered directly 'off the drawing board'.

No 600 took their Demons for a brief spell at Kenley before returning to Hendon on 4th October 1938. No 601 on the other hand had converted from the Demon to the Gloster Gauntlet II, the last of the open cockpit fighter biplanes to serve with the RAF. They were the fastest fighters in service from 1935 until 1937 and at the last RAF display at Hendon in that year, Gauntlets of No 66 Squadron took over the role of formation aerobatics from the Bristol Bulldog. These were the great days of service flying and every year on the air display days, the people would flock to Hendon to see the RAF fly. Though still equipped with obsolescent biplanes, the speed of the aircraft and the dare-devil flying of the pilots would thrill them every year. However, the signs of another conflict approaching were on everyone's mind and very shortly, there would be no more of the famous Hendon air displays.

If the auxiliaries appeared to be converting to different aircraft, there was no comparison between them and No 24 Squadron. Up until March 1935, communication flights had been carried out mainly in military and training aircraft of all types. In 1937, a DH89A and a DH86B were received for VIP use but with this mixture of aircraft, it was planned to standardise the squadron with the Miles Mentor. The advent of war however changed all this and 24 Squadron received another mixture of aircraft for its purpose. These included Dragon Rapides, Magisters, Ansons, Electras and many more. Never had a squadron used so many different types.

On 10th February 1936, No 611 (West Lancashire) Auxiliary Squadron formed at Hendon. Commanded by Squadron Leader G.L. Pilkington and flying the Hawker Hart, they left for Liverpool and Speke two months later, not to return. Not so 600 and 601 who, in October 1938, converted to the then modern Bristol Blenheim. They both received the mark IF which was used in a night-fighter role and also for early experiments in airborne radar. Whilst at Hendon, all three auxiliary units worked up on their new aircraft but with the war now very imminent, 600 moved over to Northolt, 601 to Biggin Hill and 604 to North Weald leaving Hendon with No 24 Squadron. Another squadron to receive the Blenheim was No 248 who reformed at the base on 30th October 1939. They too worked up on the type at Hendon before leaving for North Coates in February 1940 to become part of Coastal Command.

On the eve of war, the London Air Raid System was tested. Plainly audible at Hendon, the men and women stood and listened, realising that this was a sound which would soon become all too familiar. The broadcast by the Prime Minister, Neville Chamberlain on 3rd September 1939 brought home the reality of war. The Czech surrender had not brought a permanent peace to Britain. It had just bought us time to test our defences and to gather further the arms with which to fight the enemy.

What was not known at this time was just how fast the German war machine would sweep across Europe.

The Phoney War had little impact on Hendon, it was still used for communications work and for keeping desk-bound pilots current in flying. No 248 Squadron were still busy getting to know their new aircraft and even the new year and the increasing attacks on Channel convoys did nothing to disturb the routine of Hendon. It played no part in the Dunkirk evacuation but just prior to this, the airfield did assume the role of a fighter station – just! No 257 (Burma) Squadron had seen action during the First World War as an anti-submarine seaplane unit. Disbanded in 1919, it reformed at Hendon on 17th May 1940 as a fighter squadron equipped with Spitfire Is. It commenced working up on the aircraft and had actually got to the air-firing stage of training when the Spitfires were taken away for another squadron. They were replaced by Hurricane Is which again required a further period of training. By 1st July, under the

Air to air photo of a Stuka over a Channel convoy. (RAF Northolt)

70

In 1940, the inhabitants of Hendon contributed money towards the purchase of four Spitfires, one of which was named 'Hendon Lamb' and was flown by No 303 Polish Squadron. A lamb holding the cross of St George forms part of the Hendon Borough Crest. (DP Baker)

command of Squadron Leader Bayne, they were deemed operational but were posted to Northolt on the 4th, leaving Hendon once again with No 24 Squadron.

As high summer approached, the skies above south-eastern England became criss-crossed with vapour trails, evidence of fierce dog-fighting taking place. Hendon, with no regular fighter squadrons, was spared much of this action. As the battle passed through its various stages and September arrived, the ferocity of the Luftwaffe attacks on the radar stations and airfields of 11 Group increased. With further squadrons needed to combat the enemy, No 504 (County of Nottingham) Auxiliary Squadron were ordered south from Catterick. Having fought in France as part of the BEF, they were no strangers to combat and a chance to hit back at the enemy down south was just what they wanted. Commanded by Squadron Leader J. Sample, DFC, they left Catterick and brought their Hurricanes down to Hendon on 6th September 1940.

71

Prior to this, the Luftwaffe had tried every method to entice the RAF into the air, and, with their superior numbers of aircraft, had hoped to clear the way for a sea and air invasion. This as yet had not happened and there were some in the German High Command who said that only by bombing London into submission would the way be clear. By accident, some enemy aircraft had already dropped their bombs on the outer suburbs of London, but September was to see this amount increase, and not by accident.

By 7th September, the decision had been reached by the enemy that indeed, London was to become the prime target. The Air Ministry had for some time been worried that an invasion was imminent and had taken the precaution of issuing 'a state of readiness' notice:

Invasion Alert No 3 – an attack is probable within three days.
Invasion Alert No 2 – an attack is probable within two days.
Invasion Alert No 1 – an attack is imminent.

As Saturday 7th September dawned fair with some early morning haze, the personal train of Reichmarschall Goering drew to a stop along the Pas-de-Calais. He had personally taken command of the new assault upon London and wanted to see his bombers leaving the French coast and heading towards England. As the masses of aircraft passed overhead, Fighter Command prepared for the onslaught. With the radar and Observer Corps plotting their course, it was realised that the target this time was to be London. No 504 were on stand-by at Hendon and were scrambled around 3.30 pm to protect the capital. They met the enemy head-on and a furious battle began with the result that many German aircraft did not return home that afternoon. Their wrecks littered the south-east as far up as the London suburbs. No 504 lost one Hurricane, that of Flying Officer K.V. Wendel who baled out but later sadly died of his horrific burns and injuries. His aircraft, L1615, crashed at Sandbanks Farm near Faversham at 5 pm. Another Hurricane, P3021, was forced to land at Eastchurch with Sergeant B.M. Bush unhurt.

The next few days saw further attacks on London both by day and by night. Hitler had planned Operation Sealion, the invasion of England, to commence on 24th September, conditions permitting. He had set high hopes on the bombing of London and had predicted that by the autumn, he would be in the capital city.

No 504 saw further action on Wednesday, 11th September when they sadly lost Pilot Officer A.W. Clarke. Flying Hurricane P3770, he was shot down in combat over the Kent coast at 4 pm. His aircraft crashed at Newchurch on Romney Marsh, but no signs of the pilot were ever found. In an earlier action, 504 also had two further Hurricanes damaged but repairable.

The next two days saw cloud and rain over the British Isles resulting in a reduced effort by the Luftwaffe. Even so, London was still burning and from Hendon it was easy to see the huge dense cloud that hung over the capital. Every now and then an explosion rent the air as gas mains and delayed action bombs exploded. Hitler was pleased with the results so far, relying on the evidence that his High Command presented. In actual fact, the Luftwaffe had lost many aircraft and still had not gained the superiority in the air that they needed. Although London was burning, the situation was not right for 'Sealion'. Consequently, at a gathering of his Chiefs of Staff on 14th September, Hitler postponed the invasion until 17th September.

The night of the 14th saw reduced activity over London due to local thunderstorms. By the morning of Sunday, 15th September, the bad weather had moved on and across the Channel, the Luftwaffe was preparing for its final thrust to bring Fighter Command and the country to its knees. By dawn, the reconnaissance Heinkels were airborne to report on weather conditions for the assault that was to follow. By 11 am, the radar stations were warning Stanmore of large formations crossing the Channel. No 11 Group readied eleven squadrons, one of them 504 at Hendon. As Squadron Leader Sample DFC led his Hurricanes to meet the enemy, the weather was so clear that, from their height, they could see the Kent and Sussex coastline. Their task however was to defend the capital far below and, warning his pilots to watch out for the fighters protecting the bombers, Sample and 504, together with other squadrons, went into the battle.

They found that they did not have to worry about the protecting fighters for with their limited fuel endurance, they had to leave the bombers and return to France. Even so, there were still problems as Sergeant R.T. Holmes in P2725 soon found out. Coming up behind a Do 17, he exhausted most of his ammunition in seconds without seeing the aircraft go down. Frustrated, he turned away just as a second Do 17 came within his sights. Realising that he had very little with which to attack, impulsively he closed on the Dornier and fired the rest of his ammunition.

Coming in a little too close, it appeared as though the two aircraft touched, causing his Hurricane to go out of control. Baling out, Sergeant Holmes watched his Hurricane crash somewhere near Chelsea. The Dornier plunged to its death, with part of it crashing into Victoria Station. During its descent, the aircraft broke into several pieces with the rear fuselage containing the body of Uffz Gustav Audel falling on Fulham town. Two further crew members, Oblt Zehbe and Uffz Goschenhofer were also killed with Uffz Hammermeister and Obergefr Armbruster captured. Coming down gently over Chelsea, Sergeant Holmes realised that he was going to land on the roof of a Chelsea house and attempting to adjust his rate of descent, clipped the guttering of the house and promptly landed in a dustbin.

Other 504 Squadron aircraft were lost in the same sortie. Hurricane N2468 was shot down and crashed into a house at Hartley in Kent sadly killing Pilot Officer J.V. Gurteen, whilst Hurricane L1913 flown by Flight Lieutenant E.A. Royce returned to Hendon badly damaged but repairable. The rest of the squadron returned to Hendon and were once again in the air shortly after as another large formation headed for London.

Again, the enemy suffered badly at the hands of Fighter Command with Do 17z (3457) being shot down by the CO, Squadron Leader Sample, and crashing onto Barnehurst Golf Club near Dartford at 2.45 pm. Three of the crew, Uffz Burballa, Flgr Bormann and Uffz Hansburg were killed in the crash with Lt Michaelis being captured. Several more fell to the Hurricanes of 504 but sadly, Flying Officer M. Zebo crashed near Dartford. He suffered very bad burns and later died in Dartford Hospital.

For the enemy, the day that was intended to bring London and

74

A popular postcard commemorating Dowding and the Battle of Britain. (Border Arts)

the country to its knees had failed. The Luftwaffe losses were higher on this day than any since the 18th August, although they had devastated large areas of Battersea, Camberwell, Lewisham and Lambeth. One aircraft even managed to bomb Buckingham Palace, or at least the lawn at the rear of the palace! Their Majesties were not in residence at the time. That night the news bulletins were full of stories of success. '185 enemy aircraft shot down', roared the headlines. Though this figure was exaggerated, the Luftwaffe had suffered grievously. Fighter Command had lost 26 aircraft with 13 pilots saved. It was still a dreadful loss of life but the balance was beginning to change in favour of the RAF.

The 16th proved a quiet day but on the 17th, 504 sadly lost Sergeant D.A. Helcke when he lost control of his aircraft following a dummy attack by RAF fighters over Faversham.

75

Baling out, he fell into the path of another aircraft and was killed. He was buried with full military honours at Herne Bay. It was a sad day, and was the last one whilst stationed at Hendon as the squadron moved to Filton on 26th September.

Over this period, the station had come to the attention of the Luftwaffe. Though the damage to the airfield was minimal, one attack on 25th September caused considerable damage within the area and some civilian deaths, but with the departure of 504, it appeared as though the enemy had recognised that Hendon did not present a threat. 'Sealion' however was postponed until the spring of 1941. With the bad weather setting in and the hours of daylight getting less, plus the non-co-operation of the RAF in being cleared from the skies of south-east England, it was felt by Hitler that perhaps the constant night bombing would bring defeat.

For Hendon, although no permanent units were based there, it was still a busy time. Towards the end of 1940, No 1 Camouflage Unit arrived operating a variety of aircraft. Their sole task was to test the effectiveness of airfield camouflage, a not very glamorous but highly specialised job for the pilots and observers. They stayed until 1942 when their job was completed and with the war being taken back to Europe, were not really necessary.

On 11th November 1940, the Luftwaffe returned to bomb Hendon, placing bombs both in the east and west side of the camp. Whilst some damage was done, it in no way hampered the running of the station. 1941 saw No 24, the communications squadron, still in residence. An Army Co-Operation Flight, No 1416, brought its Spitfires in on 3rd March to fly in collaboration with the local Ack-Ack units. Changing their Spitfires for Blenheims in the summer of 1941, they moved to Benson in the autumn.

No 1416 were joined on 24th April by an unusual unit, No 116. They had been formed in February from No 1 Anti-Aircraft Calibration Flight with Westland Lysanders, their main task being the calibration of predictors and AA radar used by the numerous Ack-Ack batteries around England. The squadron was dispersed at several airfields and with its motto 'Precision in Defence' proving very apt, it carried out sterling work until a move to Heston on 20th April 1942, by then adding Hurricanes to its inventory.

The rest of 1941 was carried out in similar vein with all the different units working to capacity. Though no more fighter units were to be based there, Hendon continued to play a very important part in the war effort. No 1 Camouflage Unit moved to Stapleford Tawney on 1st June 1942 whilst No 510 formed at Hendon from a nucleus of No 24 on 15th October, taking over some of the aircraft of No 24 Squadron. Like the latter, it was a communications unit flying a varied selection of aircraft such as Tiger Moths, Ansons and Proctors. The remainder of 1942 saw very little change at Hendon, either in units or usage.

The long term strategy for the base was that it would eventually become a transport airfield, the first indications of this change becoming evident on 18th June 1943 when No 512 Squadron formed, and Hendon became a unit in 44 Group, Transport Command. No 512 were soon equipped with the Douglas Dakota, by far the most celebrated of all transport aircraft. Over 1,200 Dakotas were supplied to the RAF under the Lease/Lend Act with America, the type eventually remaining in service with the RAF until 1949/50. Flights to Gibraltar and North Africa were started immediately, these eventually taking the form of scheduled services for VIPs and the movement of troops. The squadron remained at Hendon until 14th February 1944 when they moved to Broadwell and began to train for D-Day. They did however leave a nucleus of personnel behind which formed No 575 Squadron at Hendon on 1st February and again, equipped with Dakotas, they too moved to Broadwell to join 512 Squadron on 14th February 1944.

Hendon was to play no part in the D-Day landings other than flying the top brass to and from important meetings connected with the invasion. No 510 Squadron was redesignated the Metropolitan Communications Squadron on 8th April 1944 and together with No 24, carried on in a communications role. 1944 was also to see an Air Despatch and Reception Unit form at Hendon. Large aircraft such as Dakotas, Yorks and B-17s were to be seen side by side with aircraft of the newly formed BOAC. The heavier aircraft brought their own problems and it was found necessary to place metal tracking over the grass, similar to Sommerfeld Tracking used on the Advanced Landing Grounds in Kent and Sussex but stronger.

Dakota I FD 772 seen operating with No 24 (Communications) Squadron at Hendon in March 1943. (MOD via B Robertson)

A reminder of enemy action came back to Hendon in June 1944 when a V1 Flying Bomb struck Colindale Hospital killing four airmen. Again in August, a V1 landed directly on the airfield destroying a barrack block and five accommodation huts. In this one incident, five men were killed and a further 25 injured. Though intended to come down directly on London, many of the V1s and later the V2s came down to the north of the capital. With the aiming point for the V1s the Tower of London, a total of 5,735 robots had been launched against the capital by 2nd August. In the last week of the month only 37 V1s reached London as the sites of the launching pads were overrun by the advancing Allies.

Towards the end of 1944, Hendon was indeed a very busy airfield. In addition to its transport and communications duties, it housed a Bomb Disposal Unit, two training schools and the RAF Regiment. At the same time it ceased to be administered by No 44 Group and became part of ACC No 16 Wing. This usage continued until the end of the war in 1945 and well into peacetime. Not until 25th February 1946 did 24 Squadron move

78

A fine photograph of Hendon showing the various hangars and messes.
(PHT Green)

to Bassingbourne, after their lengthy stay, leaving the Metropolitan Communications Squadron to continue their role.

Peace also brought the reforming of No 601 (County of London) and No 604 (County of Middlesex) Auxiliary Squadrons. Both were flying Spitfires, remaining at Hendon until March 1949 when they moved over to North Weald. The first Americans to use the airfield arrived in 1946 when a new Navy Transport Unit, VRU-4 was established. Flying DC3s and DC4s, they were used to ferry men and materials to and from the Mediterranean 6th Fleet. They remained for 14 years before moving to Blackbushe.

Surrounded as it was by an ever increasing encroachment of housing, there was very little room in which to expand Hendon. The new jet aircraft demanded more room and hard runways and the safety margin for airfields and nearby housing was extended. Closure, however, was not immediate. The Metropolitan Communications Squadron became No 31 Squadron, reverting back to its former name on 1st March 1955 and disbanding at Hendon before reforming at Laarbruch in Germany shortly after. Even with the departure of the one remaining flying unit, Hendon continued to be home to an Air Experience Flight for Air Cadets, the RAF Antarctic Flight and a Royal Auxiliary Air Force flight with two Austers. The famous Hendon Air Displays were reinstated, now being called the Battle of Britain Day displays.

This scenario continued until 1957 when all powered flight ceased. A unique occasion took place on 1st June 1968 when the last flight at Hendon by a fixed wing aircraft took place. A Blackburn Beverley, destined for the proposed RAF Museum, flew in amid very mixed emotions. It was soon after this that the metal runways were taken up.

It was Winston Churchill who, during the height of the Battle of Britain, wrote to the Rt Hon Sir Archibald Sinclair saying: 'I should have thought that Hendon could provide at least two good squadrons of fighter or bomber aircraft of the reserve category . . . Then they could be thrown in when an emergency came. Ought you not every day to call in question in your mind every non-military aspect of the Air Force?' Though Hendon was active during the battle, it was not on the level envisaged by the Prime Minister.

None the less, it played its part well and it was the choice of the many when it was decided to set up a national RAF Museum in 1960. It was to occupy ten acres of the original site and from the design stage to the official opening by Her Majesty The Queen on 15th November 1972, took twelve years. There is no doubt that it is the best and most comprehensive aviation museum, and is the envy of many countries the world over, including America. That it should be built at Hendon, a historic aviation site since the days of Claude Grahame-White, is an added bonus and will ensure that future generations will be able to see what a contribution the Royal Air Force has made to aviation history.

6

HESTON

The infamous piece of paper carried by Neville Chamberlain on his return from Munich is not Heston's only claim to fame for it was also the first home to photographic reconnaissance, a unit of the RAF that did much to aid the war effort. The grass airfield also became a satellite to nearby Northolt and as such was another home for many Polish squadrons. Pre-war it was a popular civil airfield, a position that it reverted to post-war. At the same time it became well known for aircraft production and servicing. No longer recognisable due to the M4 motorway slicing it in half, Heston could well have become London's main airport if fate had deemed it that way.

Lying eleven miles west of London, this flat area of vacant land first came to the notice of two men who had nowhere permanent to keep their private aircraft. In 1928, Nigel Norman and Alan Muntz, both private aviators with Norman holding a commission with No 601 (County of London) Auxiliary Squadron, were told that the Air Ministry would not allow them to keep their aircraft in the squadron hangar at Hendon. Looking in the near locality, they found an area of land near Cranford which would suit their purpose. They had the land developed as an airfield and called it Heston, after the larger of the two villages. They formed a company to raise the capital and calling it Airwork Ltd, first occupied the site in February 1929.

Heston airfield in the 1930s. A fine shot showing the unusual concrete

hangar. (Hounslow Library)

The construction of several buildings began immediately with the building of a reinforced concrete hangar. This method of construction was totally unique at the time in that it was circular and measured 80 feet by 100 feet. This together with several aeroplane sheds and a three-storied centre tower comprising club rooms, offices and a control tower positioned on the top, allowed the official opening of Heston to take place on 6th July 1929 by Lord Thompson, the then Air Minister.

It soon became a popular venue with the King's Cup Air Race being held there the same year, together with Airwork Ltd opening a flying school. The Chief Instructor was Captain V.H. Baker who later formed a company, the Martin-Baker Company in conjunction with James Martin. Though the company is now world famous for its pioneering ejection seats, Martin-Baker did produce a private venture fighter aircraft in which Baker was killed owing to an engine failure on take-off. Heston was also the

Heston's terminal building showing the control tower and clubhouse. (via P Baker)

84

base from which several pioneering long distance flights left, with aircraft production beginning when Comper Aircraft moved to Heston from Hooton Park in Cheshire in 1933. They manufactured the lovely Swift aircraft which became a firm favourite with private flyers.

At the same time, the first privately owned aviation ground radio station was installed in the control tower by Amplion Ltd, with receivers being fitted in some of the school Moths. The maximum range achieved was of the order of 30 miles but experiments were carried out with the supervision of first solo flights, when the instructor would step out of the aircraft, hurry to the tower and then stand by to talk the pupil out of any troubles that he might experience.

Scheduled passenger services operated by Spartan Airlines began with flights to Cowes on the Isle of Wight, and when Jersey Airlines commenced flying from Heston to Jersey with De Havilland Dragons in 1934, the future of the field looked assured.

Inflationary pressures, however, sadly forced the closure of Comper Aircraft that same year, but it did not disappear entirely with the assets being taken over by a newly formed company called the Heston Aircraft Company. This company produced a monoplane for private use, a design that previously had been

In 1935, Spartan Air Lines was operating Spartan Cruiser IIs and IIIs on the Heston-Isle of Wight service. Cruiser II G-ACUT was one of the aircraft used.

used mainly by De Havilland. It was known as the Heston Phoenix and the aircraft was a five-seat, high wing, cabin monoplane with a retractable undercarriage, the first fitted to this type of aircraft. Unfortunately only six were ever built, the cost of such an aircraft being exorbitant at the time.

The civil side continued to flourish when Whitehall Securities who controlled Spartan Airways formed United Airways. They also controlled Highland Airways and Northern and Scottish Airways, all of these companies being rationalised later to form Allied British Airways in September 1935, with the title eventually being shortened to British Airways Ltd a month later. Commencing operations on 1st January 1936, Heston became their main London terminal with flights all over the UK and Northern Europe. Unfortunately this happy position was to last only for six months before British Airways moved to the newly constructed Gatwick Airport. Two years later they were back at Heston after spending a year at Croydon when Gatwick was found to have a water-logging problem. This time, British Airways were to stay until the outbreak of war.

With this assurance, Heston entered a period of expansion with a new hangar being built to accommodate the larger civilian aircraft and the installation of a new Customs and Immigration hall. In March 1938, British Airways had been appointed by the Air Ministry to operate scheduled services to South America and West Africa. Originally operating the Lockheed 10A Electra aircraft, the company now looked to its successor, the Lockheed 14 in which to carry out the new service. The first arrived on 3rd September 1938 to operate the first service on the 18th in Electra G-AFGN.

The serial number is worthy of mention because it was this aircraft that carried Mr Neville Chamberlain on the second of three visits to meet Adolf Hitler in his quest for peace. Arthur Neville Chamberlain was the Conservative politician who worked his way up from being Minister of Health in 1923 to becoming Chancellor of the Exchequer in 1931. He succeeded Baldwin as Prime Minister in 1937 at a time when the war clouds were once again gathering in Europe. As Prime Minister he attempted to 'appease' the territorial demands of the European dictators, particularly Mussolini.

Heston at its busiest during the 1930s. (via P Baker)

Noticeably worried by the situation, he flew to Germany from Heston in G-AFGN on 15th September 1938 to meet Hitler with the knowledge that the general feeling from the majority of men in the country was that he should defy Hitler even if it meant war whilst the majority of women thought he should continue to appease him. He landed back at Heston the same evening with no news and returned for a further meeting with Hitler at Bad Godesberg on 22nd September, G-AFGN again departing from Heston. Yet again he returned empty handed to Heston but on 28th September, whilst in Parliament, he was handed a note. Hitler had requested a further meeting.

Once again, on 1st October, the aircraft took him to Germany. This time at the meeting the Czechs were persuaded to surrender the Sudetenland to Germany and when Mr Chamberlain returned to Heston a battery of microphones awaited his arrival. As he stepped down from the aircraft he held aloft a piece of paper in his hand and later declared, 'I believe it is peace for our time.' As history records, the Czech solution did not bring peace, only much needed time.

Despite all the comings and goings of Chamberlain, Heston continued in its role as a civilian airfield. A regular visitor to the airfield was an Australian named Sidney Cotton. He was already known to the military for his work in designing the Sidcot Suit, worn by the pilots of the RFC. Travelling all over the world, his business was photography and with the realisation that another global war was about to break, Sidney Cotton came into contact with the British Secret Service. He was approached to see if he would help with a joint Anglo-French venture to photograph German military installations. After agreeing terms, Cotton said yes and two Lockheed 12s were made available to him together with a cover-up phoney company named the Aeronautical Research and Sales Corporation.

The unit first flew from an airfield near Paris and then from Tunis but difficulties in working with the French forced Cotton to return to the UK. Back home he sought an interview with Arthur Tedder, who was then the Director General of Research and Development for the Air Ministry, telling him that photographic reconnaissance would have a big impact on the outcome of the approaching war. Tedder was persuaded and allowed Cotton to sell the two Lockheed 12s to the French and then purchase his own aircraft. G-AFTL arrived at Heston and was extensively modified by Airwork. With additional fuel tanks and hidden cameras built into the fuselage, Cotton first took the aircraft to the Middle East in June 1939 in order to photograph Italian military installations.

Despite the obvious rumblings of war, Heston once again began a period of expansion on the civil side. Plans were drawn up for new hangars, terminal and other buildings together with an expansion of the airfield itself. Another 178 acres were added to its dimensions, making it one of the largest grass airfields of the time. British Airways were still opening new routes despite the tensions but the news that the Germans had marched into Poland stopped all further plans. The requisitioning of Heston by the Air Ministry in September 1939 forced British Airways to move their operations to Bristol as the airfield was deemed a satellite airfield to Northolt in No 11 Group, Fighter Command.

Another view of busy Heston during the run-up to war. (via P Baker)

With the departure of British Airways, Heston seemed strangely quiet. The club aircraft were either flown elsewhere or placed into a hangar, with some private aircraft being retained by the National Air Communication Organisation. The Phoney War period allowed the airfield to organise itself onto a war footing, this being further accentuated by a decision of the Air Ministry to form a photographic flight.

For some time, Sidney Cotton had been suggesting to the Ministry that his photographic work continued but on a military basis. The RAF were experiencing problems with their photo-reconnaissance flights and the series of meetings between Cotton and the Ministry came at a very opportune moment. The RAF cameras suffered from condensation on the lenses in the low temperatures at high altitudes. Cotton's knowledge enabled him to overcome this by allowing warm air from the engine to flow via a ducting around the cameras. It was not long before the Air Ministry began to acknowledge his expertise and he was given the go-ahead to form a unit. On 22nd September 1939, the Heston

Flight was formed with Sidney Cotton being given the rank of Wing Commander. It was felt necessary to include a subterfuge name for the flight and after some deliberation it was called 'No 2 Camouflage Unit' on 3rd November 1939.

Wing Commander Cotton had requested a pair of Spitfires but with such a limited number at that time, he was given instead a pair of Bristol Blenheims. Airwork took them in and adapted them for his purposes but they proved totally inadequate. Again the very persuasive Cotton went to the C-in-C Fighter Command, Air Chief Marshal Dowding, with the result that two new Spitfires were allocated to the flight. Once again, Airwork adapted them by taking out all the guns, fittings and armour plating then fitting additional fuel tanks to allow their range to be increased. And increased it was, with the aircraft now capable of flying 1,250 miles compared with the normal range of 395 miles.

Cotton also gathered together the best team possible for his flight and on 5th November 1939, the first sortie was flown from the French airfield of Seclin. Spitfire N3071, flown by Flight Lieutenant 'Shorty' Longbottom, DFC, took a series of first class photos of the Aachen area of Germany from 33,000 feet. The films were immediately flown to Heston for processing, the information they provided proving that the decision to form the flight had been the right one. The use of Spitfires was not, however, without its dramas. Heston in those days was without runways and the camera-loaded Spitfires would have two groundcrew sitting on the tail during a taxi out for take-off across the bumpy grass. With the engine running up at the take-off point, both men would then clamber underneath the fuselage and clean the mud and grass from the glass camera apertures prior to take-off.

In one instance the pilot was a young Belgian sergeant who, despite his limited understanding of English, professed to understand the instructions not to move until signalled by the two airmen underneath that all was clear. He had recently arrived from a fighter squadron and he continued to operate as a fighter pilot by immediately turning into the wind to take off. One of the men on the tail sensed what was happening and jumped off. His companion stayed on and with his forage cap over his face (common practice on engine testing) and his arm hooked around the fin, was apparently unaware he was about to leave the ground.

The aircraft climbed in short, sharply inclined steps to about 1,000 feet. Realising that all was not well, the pilot steered a half circuit and attempted to land. In doing so, he lowered his undercarriage and complicated the aircraft's instability. The resultant impact parted the undercarriage and airframe, the aircraft bounced twice and broke its back. The airman, still crouched on the rear and terrified, shot off and rolled like a ball in the mud. Both he and the pilot were unhurt but when the pilot finally understood what had happened, he fainted on the spot. Wing Commander Geoffrey Tuttle, the CO, was not amused but no charges were forthcoming. There was however a tightening up of procedures!

The Christmas of 1939 saw the entire country covered in snow. For a period all sorties were cancelled, but such had been the success of the Heston Flight that it was given the official title of 'The Photographic Development Unit' and was allocated further pilots and aircraft. Now operating solely from Heston, the Spitfires were used in good weather whilst the new Hudsons were used when visibility was poor. January and February 1940 saw operations continue with a first being achieved by Flight Lieutenant Bob Niven when he flew the first Spitfire sortie over the Ruhr from Heston on 2nd March 1940.

Despite the opening phases of the war, the Heston Aircraft Company had quietly been designing a new aircraft. It was to be a racing aircraft which it was hoped would take the world's landplane speed record, at that time held by a Messerschmitt Bf 113R with a speed of 379.6 mph. Named the Heston Napier Racer, it was to be powered by the then new Napier Sabre engine. With one prototype built and another in process, Squadron Leader G.L.G. Richmond, the pilot, waited for favourable conditions to test fly the aircraft.

The day arrived, 12th June 1940, with everyone having high hopes for the success of the aircraft. Running up the large and as yet virtually untried engine, Richmond taxied to the runway and having checked his instruments, took off, having filed a 30 minute flight plan. Within seconds the Racer became airborne prematurely when it hit a large bump in the grass. Continuing his climb, Richmond noticed that his engine was overheating badly, possibly due to a glycol connection being broken as the result of the bump. Completing a circuit and in some considerable pain due to the scalding steam from the engine, Squadron Leader Richmond levelled off and stalled at a height of 20 to 30 feet. The Racer in hitting the ground, broke off the landing gear and the tail. Luckily the pilot escaped with cuts and bruises and was only badly shaken up but for the company, it was a failed dream. The second prototype was never completed and no further designs were forthcoming. The Napier Sabre engine was later fitted to the very successful range of Typhoon and Tempest aircraft from Hawkers though they too, found early problems with the engine overheating.

With the Battle of Britain being fought in the skies above, no call was made upon Heston to accommodate fighter squadrons. It was however still a very busy station with many movements. Although not classed as military aircraft, several civil aircraft, both British and foreign, were taken over by the RAF for communications and transport duties. At Heston, this even included the Heston Phoenix which was used in a communications role for some time.

The photographic unit had continued its valuable work into the new year. Still further modifications were made to the Spitfires and, in order to make interception even more difficult, they had been painted in a very pale shade of duck-egg green. Wing Commander Cotton called it 'Camotint'. After the painting the Spitfires had been carefully polished to reduce drag to a minimum. Yet still more range could be squeezed out of the aircraft when extra fuel was carried in the hollow leading edge of the wings. Early in 1940, a new long-range version of the Spitfire came from the Supermarine stable. Previous Spitfires had been designated 'IA' and 'IB' but now the Spitfire PRIC had arrived for the PDU. This had a 30 gallon fixed blister tank under the port wing with a similarly shaped blister under the starboard wing. This, however, did not contain fuel but a pair of F.24 cameras with 8 inch focal length lenses. With an additional fuel tank behind the pilot, the PRIC gave the range to roam over Germany. If proof were needed, on 7th April 1940, Kiel was photographed for the first time.

On 10th February 1940, No 212 Squadron was reformed at Heston, the first pure RAF squadron to use the airfield. It had disbanded on 9th February 1920 and was reformed to join the PDU to carry out strategic photographic reconnaissance duties over France. The surviving personnel and aircraft arrived at Heston but a detachment was immediately sent to France where Blenheims replaced the Spitfires. After flying several missions, they were forced to evacuate the French airfield on 16th June and return to Heston. During June, the PDU was for some reason transferred to Coastal Command and in July was renamed the Photographic Reconnaissance Unit. Whilst it made no difference to the day to day running of the unit, the complement of aircraft increased to eight Spitfire Mk.Is.

The airfield first came to the attention of the Luftwaffe on Monday, 26th August. A cloudy but dry day, it was a day of many raids on the 11 Group airfields. With Debden, Hornchurch and Northolt airfields receiving heavy raids and with Heston just a short distance away, several raiders strayed from the main formation, spotted Heston below and unleashed their bombs. Apart from the grass landing area being cratered, very little damage was done. Not so in the raids that took place during September. With the attacks, both day and night, now concentrating on London and the cities, it was obvious that Heston, so near to London, would not remain unscathed. The 17th September saw a further light raid on the airfield but the night of Tuesday the 19th brought fear and destruction to Heston.

Heavy raids during the previous day had lulled the military into thinking that the 19th was to be a little quieter. In fact, only 70 enemy aircraft had crossed the English coastline all day. With rain setting in as dusk fell, it was assumed that enemy raids would again be light. The weather however did not stop the Luftwaffe despatching over 200 aircraft to lay mines in the coastal waters of the Channel. A few aircraft strayed inland and had reached the suburbs of London by just after midnight. One particular aircraft overflew Heston and decided to drop its deadly mine. Whether or not the pilot really judged his target very well or dropped it at random will never be known. Whichever, the mine exploded on contact with one of the hangars containing five Spitfires of the PRU. It also contained the Lockheed 12A of the PRU together with a Wellington bomber. When the dust finally settled, it was found a total of 17 aircraft were either wrecked or damaged. There were also several injuries but luckily no loss of life.

The next morning the extent of the damage became visible. The entire roof of the hangar had collapsed together with most of the surrounding buildings. What remained of the aircraft was buried beneath metal, wood, brick and corrugated sheeting. Most of the personnel were put to clearing the rubble, an operation that went on for several days. Though the following night saw a further raid on London, Heston was left alone. It was however this bad raid and several smaller ones in October and November that finally persuaded the Air Ministry that Heston was becoming a dangerous place for a valuable unit such as the PRU. Accordingly, orders were received to move the PRU away from Heston and the London blitz to the safety of Benson in Oxfordshire. This was accomplished by 27th December 1940 leaving Heston a relatively quiet base.

Shortly after the new year, the airfield was transferred from 11 Group to 81 Group (Training). By 20th February 1941, No 53 OTU had arrived with Wing Commander J.T. (Ira) Jones, DSO, MC, DFC, MM, commanding. A legend in his own right from his exploits during the First World War, the signal to him from the Air Ministry was to get the OTU up and running as soon as possible to be ready for a move to a more permanent base at Llandow in Wales. Several Spitfires and a few Miles Masters arrived to allow the first course to begin in March. Several courses later, the OTU left Heston to be replaced on 20th February 1941 by No 61 OTU to carry on similar work.

Being training units, it was obvious that incidents would occur and they certainly did, with several Spitfires destroyed in the process. One, however, must rank as the worst and the most tragic whilst 61 OTU were at Heston.

The No 3 course had within its ranks a Belgian sergeant pilot. On 28th August 1941, having completed several training circuits, he prepared to land his Spitfire. Unfortunately he did not see a taxiing Miles Master also within the grass landing area and promptly landed his Spitfire on the top of it, killing both crew members of the Master and seriously injuring himself. After a spell in hospital, he eventually joined No 6 course and whilst taxiing his Spitfire on 6th November, another pilot made the same mistake and landed a Spitfire on top of his. On this occasion, sadly, the Belgian pilot was killed.

At the same time that these tragic incidents were taking place, a new and rather unusual unit had formed at Heston. The idea for such a unit came during the dark nights of the latter part of 1940 when it was found practically impossible to detect and shoot down enemy aircraft. Several different types of aircraft were tried in the night-fighter role, most of them achieving very little success. With electronic airborne interception still in the development stage, thoughts were turning to more manual forms of detection.

Among the variety of suggestions forthcoming was one submitted by Wing Commander W. Helmore. He was attached to the Ministry of Aircraft Production and had been working on his idea for some time. It entailed fitting an enormous and powerful searchlight in the nose of a fast bomber-type aircraft with which to illuminate the enemy aircraft. An accompanying fighter aircraft would, hopefully, shoot the enemy down. In principle a good idea, but sadly it did not work out so well as planned.

No 1422 Air Target Illumination Flight was formed at Heston under the command of Wing Commander A.E. Clouston. The first modified Douglas Havoc, the aircraft chosen to carry the light, was delivered from the Burtonwood Aircraft Repair Depot near Liverpool on 23rd April 1941. AW400 had been fitted with

A Turbinlite Havoc as flown at Heston. The large searchlight and radar array can be seen in the nose. (RAF Museum)

the early version of Airborne Interception radar and carried a searchlight that consumed 140 kilowatts. The carbon arc lamp also consumed 1,400 amps at 105 arc volts but the airborne version was to be powered by batteries. Thus the light would only be capable of four illuminations of 30 seconds before recharging would be necessary. The first failure of the idea was becoming apparent. Despite this, tests went ahead but during May 1941, the Ford airfield-based Fighter Interception Unit, carrying out an assessment of the Havoc as a suitable parent aircraft, suggested that it was too slow and not manoeuvrable enough to do the job. The Mosquito was put forward as a replacement but at that time they were needed elsewhere.

Over the coming weeks, six Havocs a week were converted at Burtonwood. The Havoc I was followed by the Havoc II with the Douglas Boston II light bomber also being converted to the Havoc configuration. By the end of July, the first ten aircraft had been completed and the operational organisation was in the process of being made up. The first flight to form was No 1451 at Hunsdon. Later on a further nine flights were formed, each one being a parent to a Defiant or Hurricane squadron. Training in all these flights took until February 1942 with the Havoc and fighter getting airborne, formating with each other until given a vector by the ground controller indicating an enemy aircraft. With the airborne radar bringing the two aircraft close to the enemy, the searchlight was switched on, hopefully with the enemy caught in its glare. It was then up to the fighter to attack. With Heston as the main training airfield, the Turbinlites went to war.

Unfortunately, the idea fell short of its expectations. There were numerous accidents with considerable loss of life. For a strength of 31 Havoc II and 39 Havoc If Turbinlites, from April to September 1942, one enemy aircraft was destroyed, one probably destroyed and two damaged. Against this, the Turbinlite squadrons lost many aircraft, both parent and satellite, with a dreadfully high loss of good crews. By September 1942, the Turbinlite days were numbered due to their ineffectiveness. Even so, Heston and 1422 Flight were still experimenting with the idea, this time using a Mosquito. Nothing came of the trials and the entire Turbinlite episode passed into the history books as a total failure.

In April 1942, the role of Heston changed yet again. It reverted back to an operational station in No 11 Group, Fighter Command. Commanded by Wing Commander H.P. Johnson and still a grass airfield, the Air Ministry decided to base one of the Northolt Polish squadrons at Heston. In flew No 316 (Warsaw) Squadron led by Squadron Leader A. Gabszewicz. It was just a short flight from Northolt to Heston, with the time from arriving on 22nd April 1942 to their first sortie a few days later being spent in settling in. There followed a fairly hectic period of Rhubarbs and Ramrods before the squadron was joined by No 302 (Poznanski) who flew their Spitfire Vbs in from Warmwell on 7th May. It was a relatively short stay for both squadrons with 302 departing to Croydon on 30th June and 316 moving to Hutton Cranswick one month later.

At this time, Heston was a very busy airfield. The Polish squadrons had been joined by No 116 Radar Calibration Squadron equipped with Westland Lysanders. The main task of this unit was the calibration of Predictors and AA Radar used by the Ack-Ack guns in the UK. Arriving on 20th April 1942, they were to remain until 12th December 1943 before moving over to Croydon.

Some of the pilots and ground crew of No 302 Polish Squadron at Heston during 1942. (P Baker)

97

With trolley acc connected, a Spitfire, W 3902 of No 302 Polish Squadron, is fired up at Heston in 1942. (RAF Northolt)

No 302 returned for a further stay on 7th July, joined on the 30th of the month by No 308 (Krakowski) Squadron. Both units were carrying out Rhubarbs and Ramrods and on 19th August 1942, took part in the ill-fated Dieppe operation (see Northolt). Over these few days, 56 fighter squadrons were engaged including five Polish. Both 302 and 308 were witness to the tragedy as they flew overhead on numerous sorties. Out of a total of 87 enemy aircraft shot down over this period, the Polish squadrons shot down 15 and shared one for the loss of two of their own. Out of the total of 2,399 sorties flown by all squadrons, they flew 224.

These were hectic days at Heston. With Dieppe over, both Polish squadrons remained until September when 302 and 308 went to Ipswich, another large grass airfield. Both returned to Heston for a further stay in late September with 308 finally leaving on 29th October to return to Northolt and 302 remaining until early 1943 when it went to Kirton-in-Lindsey.

It was a change of command at Heston as well with Wing

Commander Johnson handing the reins over to Wing Commander A.L. Mortimer, and Wing Commander S. Brzezina becoming the Polish Station Commander. It says much about these squadrons at Northolt and Heston that, on 31st December 1942, the 500th and 501st enemy aircraft were shot down by Flying Officers Pietrzak and Langhamer respectively. During the year the total sorties flown by the Poles was 10,390, this accumulating 15,365 flying hours with a total score of 90 enemy aircraft shot down, 36 probables and 43 damaged.

1943 opened with a meeting on 14th January at Casablanca between Roosevelt, Churchill and the French General Giraud. The main point of the meeting was to discuss the strong concentration in the UK of American and British land and air forces which were to prepare for a re-entry into Europe as soon as possible.

Once again, the Polish squadrons were rotated through Heston and Northolt. In addition, No 515 Squadron, which had flown in

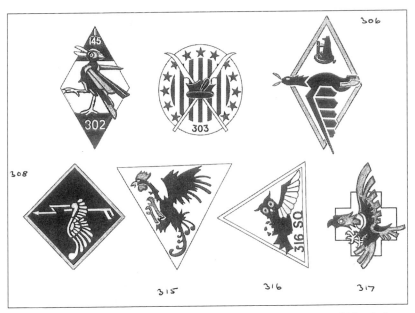

Polish squadron crests carried on aircraft fuselages at Heston and Northolt.
(C Samson)

on 29th October 1942, was operating Defiants used for jamming enemy radars. The operation was called 'Moonshine' and entailed the Defiants flying ahead of a bomber stream to jam the enemy radar transmissions. Later in 1943, the Defiants were exchanged for the Bristol Beaufighter, a far more stable platform for that type of work. No 515 left for Hunsdon on 31st May 1943, eventually to join No 100 Group in a similar role.

For five days in March, No 350 (Belgian) Squadron were at Heston prior to moving into Debden but apart from this brief change of unit, the pattern of rotations for the Poles continued. That was until the arrival of an American unit in May saw Heston enter a rather unusual period. The 2008th Army Air Force Headquarters and the Headquarters Squadron Transport Group had been established at the base in early February 1943 but was disbanded in April. Perhaps an indication of the future use of Heston, a detachment of the 27th Air Transport Group flew in from Heathrow on 7th May 1943. A communications unit used mainly for fast transportation anywhere in the UK, from August until December 1943 it recorded 598 movements. When they left just prior to Christmas, Heston prepared itself for the long awaited assault on Europe.

The 2nd Tactical Air Force was formed in preparation for the forthcoming assault. Heston was reclassified as No 133 Airfield, by which time Nos 306 and 308 Polish squadrons had returned to form part of the Northolt Wing of Spitfires. The airfield was also chosen as the base for the Allied Expeditionary Communications flight and with the turn of 1944, also became home to a new Spitfire squadron. No 129 (Mysore) Squadron flew their Spitfire IXs in from Peterhead on 16th March 1944 to join the Polish units. Many light and medium bombers were now carrying out raids on the enemy positions around the planned assault area. All three squadrons were engaged on escort sorties and even at this late stage of the war, came into frequent contact with the Luftwaffe.

As D-Day approached, the Spitfires moved to their forward bases in April leaving Heston strangely quiet. Now left as a communications base, it became home to the No 85 Group Communications Squadron. A variety of aircraft used the airfield with Oxfords, Proctors, Spitfires and Austers to be seen around

Wing Commander A.J. de Hanlik of No 308 Polish Squadron at Heston.
(P Baker)

the dispersal areas. The addition of the Heston Station Flight and a further USAAF squadron, also operating a variety of aircraft, ensured that space at the airfield was at a premium.

The 86th Air Transport Squadron, although not actually based at Heston, chose to operate from the base from January 1944. This unit flew a large range of transport aircraft including C-47s (Dakotas), all of which seemed perfectly happy departing and landing on Heston's limited grass landing area. All of this American activity ensured that the airfield lost its 11 Group status and it returned to a satellite airfield of Northolt.

The majority of 1944 was taken up by the rotation of many USAAF units through Heston. One of the more active American units was the 325th Ferrying Squadron who arrived on 11th May 1944 from Maghaberry in Northern Ireland. Flying modified B-17 Fortresses, B-24s and B-26s, they flew many transport sorties until they moved over to Northolt on 17th October. The 10th Aerodrome Squadron were another resident of the airfield and actually took over the operating of Heston from the RAF. Whilst they became responsible for the running and the defending of the airfield, they did not maintain or repair any of their aircraft. This was left to the RAF. They moved over to Grove on 7th September 1944.

With D-Day a success and the Allies beginning to push into France, in a last desperate attempt to bring the UK to its knees, Hitler unleashed his terror weapons. The first type, the V1, had first crossed the Kent coast in the early hours of Monday, 13th June. From this time, the number of launchings increased daily. With the Tower of London the intended aiming point, many fell short of the capital whilst others overshot and carried on. Such a case was when a V1 came down at Heston on 28th June. It caused considerable damage to the airfield, but the worst hit was the second V1 which crashed on Heston on 5th July. This Flying Bomb caused several deaths and even more damage just as the clearance from the first one was all but finished. Whilst the capital was to see many more V1s and the more sinister V2 rockets crash within its boundaries, Heston was spared further devastation.

The autum of 1944 saw a rapid decline in military use. A plan to develop nearby Heathrow as a major civilian airport forced the Fairey Aviation Flying Unit to look for new premises. They found Heston and hastily moved in. With most of the military aircraft, both British and American gone, they joined the Station Flight and No 1422 Flight, still resident despite the demise of the Turbinlites. The 13th January 1945 saw the airfield transferred to the Director General of Civil Aviation as Fairey Aviation began to assemble Firefly aircraft. With the addition of three extra hangars, a new look Heston began to take shape.

On 18th April 1945 the military returned in the shape of No 701 Squadron, Fleet Air Arm. This unit had been formed at Heston by expanding 'B' Flight of No 781 Squadron which had been operating from the old Fairey airfield at Heathrow. Operating under the administrative control of Lee-on-Solent, it was a communications squadron carrying VIPs and other passengers to and from the London area. Aircraft were mainly Oxfords and Travellers but Expeditors and Dominies were also flown. The unit finally disbanded at Heston on 13th January 1947.

A post-war product of the Heston works, the prototype Heston A2/45 Gipsy Queen photographed in November 1947. (Crown via B Robertson)

The Heston Napier Racer, G-AFOK. Forever portrayed in the street arches of the area.

Heston Aircraft, the original residents of the airfield, were still busy with Spitfire reconnaissance conversion work. They were further tasked with design work on the Sea Hornet and were also working on civilian aircraft conversions. However, the rapid expansion of nearby Heathrow as the main London Airport was having a detrimental effect on Heston. With the airfields so close there was a real danger of an incident occurring. Sadly, Heston was forced to close with the Fairey works moving over to White Waltham and Airwork moving out in the early 1950s. No 1422 Flight disbanded together with the Station Flight whilst the Heston Aircraft Company moved to new premises. For a time, BOAC used the hangars but the final demise came in 1965 when the new M4 motorway was constructed directly across the airfield. Part of the landing area was returned to agriculture with the control tower and adjoining buildings being pulled down in December 1978.

A few signs of its past, however, remain to be seen today. The concrete hangar, now under a preservation order, is still intact and has been put to industrial use whilst five early aircraft sheds are used for storage purposes. One old administration building is now the office of P. Lowery and Sons Ltd and pieces of the original perimeter track are still to be seen. Visible reminders of this once very active and pretty airfield are the metal street arches within the local area which incorporate the Heston Napier Racer, G-AFOK. For the rest, sadly it has been confined to the history books.

7

LITTLE HORWOOD

With a German invasion still a strong possibility in 1941, the Air Ministry drew up plans for the dispersement of fighter squadrons from their bases in the south-east of England. As luck would have it, no invasion took place but even by the end of 1941, the plans were still active to move squadrons away from the battle front should the Luftwaffe reconsider an airborne invasion. To name a few, it was proposed that Southend would move to Fairlop, Hawkinge to Lympne and West Malling and Tangmere to Middle Wallop. Refuelling would be done at Little Horwood and Wing as well as limited servicing. None of this of course happened and both Little Horwood and Wing were left to the OTUs.

Situated two miles north-east of Winslow, Little Horwood replaced Cheddington as the satellite to Wing on 3rd September 1942. It had been appreciated early in 1939 that operational bomber squadrons could not undertake to train new aircrew. It was therefore proposed by the Command that Operational Training Units be formed for this purpose. It further stated that they should be positioned away from the coast and inland, beyond the reach of any enemy aircraft. The aircraft to be used were to be mainly Ansons, Whitleys, Battles and Wellingtons with the occasional Oxford and Dominie if no others were available. A further duty imposed upon the OTUs was the art of

'Nickelling', the dropping of propaganda leaflets over France.

By 1942 the airfield was all but complete. Rubble from the war damage in London was brought by rail to the local station and then by truck to the airfield site. It was used as hardcore for the runways, dispersal areas and the roads surrounding the airfield. On 2nd September 1942, Little Horwood was deemed operational and a few Wellingtons of No 26 OTU from Wing moved in together with the OTU Gunnery Section and the 92 Group Communications Flight aircraft. It had been decided that trainee aircrew would first arrive at the parent station of Wing to crew up and that Little Horwood would be used for practising 'circuits and bumps', cross country flying and for bombing practice. The more advanced training would then be carried out at Wing.

It was the Vickers Wellington that served most of the time at Little Horwood. Making its maiden flight on 15th June 1936, it incorporated a new construction design known as the geodetic method. This was a series of metal lattice-work structures which constituted the fuselage, which was then covered in fabric. Designed by Barnes Wallis, it proved a very tough and durable method of construction, although initially it was frowned upon by certain people at the Ministry.

Workhorse of the OTUs – the Vickers Wellington. (MAP)

107

The Wellington was the backbone of Bomber Command's early night raids over Germany before the big four-engined bombers came on stream. The Wellington Mk.III first entered service in 1942 and this together with the Mk.X were the main marks to be used by the OTUs. Both marks served at Little Horwood.

Being an OTU base and far from the main battle area, there is not a lot of wartime action to record. However, as with all operational training units, there were a number of crashes with loss of life. Much of this was due to the inexperience of the crews and the fact that the aircraft were basically obsolete. In order to give an idea of what type of accidents took place, it is necessary to list just a few:

6th December 1942 – Wellington DV885 – Engine stalled on landing.

11th December 1942 – Wellington Z9622 – Aircraft stalled on final approach.

9th April 1943 – Wellington R1628 – Forced landing east of Buckingham.

8th June 1943 – Wellington BT833 – Crashed Synon Hill Farm; 3 killed.

7th August 1943 – Wellington X3790 – Crashed on town of Winslow; 17 killed.

30th December 1943 – Wellington BK491 – Crashed North End Farm, Horwood; 4 killed.

12th May 1944 – Wellington MS483 – Crashed at Marsh Gibbon; 5 injured.

7th July 1944 – Wellington LP314 – Cause not stated; 5 killed.

These are but a few of the tragic incidents recorded. One of them, the crash of Wellington X3790 on Saturday, 7th August 1943 (also mentioned in the Wing chapter) must rate as one of the worst on record.

The take-off time for the aircraft that day was at 1.25 am. Having successfully taken off from Wing, the crew were to carry out a night flying exercise within the local area. Already they had made their mark with bombing accuracy from 10,000 feet and had reached a high degree in navigation. The night flight was one of the last hurdles to overcome before becoming fully operational. During the flight, the bomb aimer discovered the 'bomb sight' was not operating and the captain decided to return to Little Horwood.

Whilst making his final approach to the airfield, the pilot, Sergeant Davies, called on the intercom that he had 'got a red' and that he was aborting the approach in order to go around again. Struggling with the controls, Davies called to the bomb aimer, Sergeant Sowter, to help him with the control column. Sadly it was to no avail, as the Wellington came in low across the town of Winslow from the west and north of the church. A wingtip struck the top of some trees in the garden of Mr H.C. Morris, followed by the undercarriage striking the roofs of the homes of Mr and Mrs C. Weston and Mrs Stonner. As it continued its tragic journey, part of the wing of the aircraft fell into the High Street. The aircraft then ploughed through part of the Chandos Arms public house and the adjoining houses on the eastern side of the High Street, finally coming to rest on four cottages which were sited to the rear of the High Street.

The landlord of the Chandos and two occupants of the house next door were killed. Of Rose Cottages, the aircraft had demolished three and severely damaged a fourth, killing ten civilians and four members of the Wellington crew. As the fires took hold, fire crews from Winslow, Stewkley, Buckingham and Aylesbury attended together with several ambulances. The dead were taken some distance away to await the undertaker whilst the local people could only stand and pray and wonder what on earth had happened to their village.

Of the crew members, only the navigator survived when he was thrown clear of the wreckage. He was taken to the RAF hospital at Halton where he was treated for his injuries and shock. The crash, having made the national newspapers the next day, was the subject of a Court of Inquiry the following Monday, 9th August 1943. The findings, which included attaching blame to the pilot, upset all the families of the crew and the navigator survivor.

On Saturday, 7th August 1993, a memorial service was held in the parish church of St Lawrence, Winslow, 50 years after the

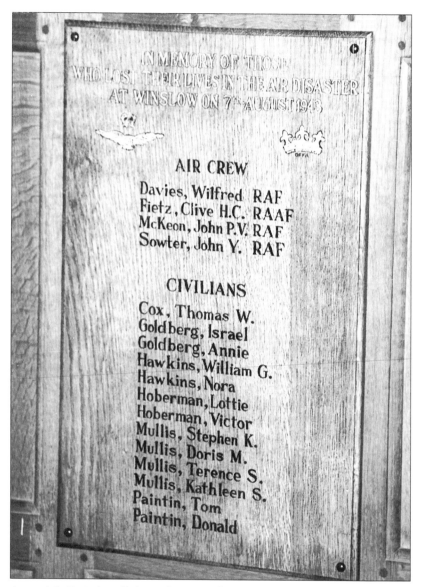

A panel dedicated to all those aircrew and civilians who lost their lives in the Winslow air crash of 7th August 1943. It rests in St Lawrence's church, Winslow. (Bert Shrimpton)

accident. During the service, a plaque was unveiled detailing the names of those who lost their lives. Amongst the congregation were survivors of the dreadful disaster. Winslow will never forget the terror of that fateful night.

No 26 OTU was not the only unit to use Little Horwood. On 5th June 1943, No 1684 Bomber Defence Training Flight formed at the station for the purpose of training OTUs in defensive tactics in accordance with a Bomber Command letter dated 6th June 1943. Several day fighter affiliation exercises were carried out using Tomahawk aircraft. Even this type of operation had its problems when on 12th July, Flight Lieutenant F.A. Bernard flying Tomahawk AH848 was involved in a taxiing accident with a crane on the perimeter. The aircraft was damaged and the incident was blamed on the steerable tail wheel becoming disiengaged. After a total of 347 exercises, the unit moved to the parent station at Wing.

No 26 OTU was to remain at Little Horwood until 26th August 1944 when it was reduced in status. This left 92 Group Communications Flight as the sole residents until November 1944 when 26 OTU regained its full status. With the end of the war, flying ceased at Little Horwood on 30th November 1945. Remnants of 26 OTU remained for several months but by January 1946, the OTU and the airfield were no longer required. Little Horwood had served its purpose admirably and had seen every aspect of war despite being so far from the front line.

8

MEMBURY

If Operation Market Garden had been the success it was hoped for, the war may well have finished one year earlier. In the words of General Montgomery, 'it could be the springboard for a powerful full-blooded thrust to the heart of Germany.' In contrast however, General Bittrich of the German Army said, 'Almost before the British had touched the ground, we were ready to defeat them.'

'Market Garden' was General Montgomery's bold and imaginative plan for an armoured and airborne thrust across Holland to outflank the German defences. After much argument, he persuaded General Eisenhower to go along with his project which incorporated the US 1st Army, the British 21st Army Group and the Allied Airborne Army. The object was to initially capture five major bridges: two over canals and three over rivers. It was an ambitious plan and if successful, the advantages could include a swift end to the war. Montgomery's aim was to drop three airborne divisions to seize the bridges on the Eindhoven-Arnhem road to enable units of the 21st Army Group to outflank the Siegfried Line. On Sunday morning, 17th September 1944, 'Market Garden' began.

The first part went well with the US 101st Airborne Division capturing the two southern bridges. At Arnhem, things had not gone right from the start. The British 1st Airborne had been dropped a long way from the town and had met fierce German resistance. The American Airborne units also found that the Nijmegen bridge was strongly held. The British Paratroops, aiming for Arnhem found their way blocked by a superior force of Germans and were eventually overwhelmed. The hoped for objective to secure a Rhine bridgehead at Arnhem had not worked according to plan and many good men were to sacrifice their lives. For Membury, whose glider units had participated fully in the invasion, it was a sad day.

As with many of the bases taken over by the Americans, Membury began life as a bomber OTU. Situated three miles south-west of Lambourn in Berkshire, it was authorised as an airfield in May 1941. It had the typical bomber airfield layout, this being a main south-west/north-east runway of 4,554 feet together with two subsidiary runways. Four T2 hangars, a technical and a domestic area completed the set-up. From the beginning it had been earmarked for Bomber Command and was in fact accepted from the contractors by No 91 Group. However, the establishment of the USAAF in the UK meant that several bomber airfields would be needed for their use, one of them being Membury. By 21st August 1942, the headquarters personnel from the 8th Group Air Support Command had arrived and designated the airfield as Station 466.

By September the units at the base comprised the 3rd Photographic Group, the 675th Observation Group and the 153rd Liaison Squadron. Quite a mixture! The aircraft used in all these roles were a few camera-equipped B-17s together with some Piper Cubs. The Photographic Unit had left by September as the first Spitfires to be flown from Membury arrived.

About a thousand Spitfires of various marks were used by units of the USAAF. The 67th Tactical Reconnaissance Group flew the Spitfire V and arrived at Membury in the autumn. Whilst the American Eagle Squadrons had flown the Spitfire during the Battle of Britain as part of Fighter Command, with the creation of the 8th Air Force, all the Eagle Squadrons became absorbed into that command.

Although the 8th had by this time established itself in the UK under the command of Major General Carl Spaatz, it was unable to accomplish much until the spring of 1943. This was due to the fact that many of the men and machines destined for the 8th were conscripted to the 12th Air Force during Operation Torch, the landings in North Africa.

Early in 1943, a number of target-towing Douglas A-20 Havocs were flown into Membury to be used in conjunction with the Spitfires. The station at this time was basically used as a training airfield and even the appearance of No 19 Squadron on 10th March 1943 with their Spitfire VBs and VCs did little to change the role. Flying in from Middle Wallop, they stayed for three days before going back to the Hampshire airfield.

In June, the unit was renamed the 67th Reconnaissance Group and with the new title came a succession of fighter sweeps over France. The Americans flew in company with the RAF on these sorties and even the Havoc crews got to go on operations when not target towing. Over the next two months, very little changed at Membury until the 67th RG moved over to Middle Wallop.

Membury was now to be extended as it became the 6th Tactical Air Depot, 9th Air Force. No further extension was possible of the main runway and so the secondary stretch running north/south was lengthened to 6,000 feet. During this work it was further decided that Membury would become the home of a Troop Carrier Group, necessitating a move from RAF control to the 9th Air Force on 22nd February 1944.

The 9th had been established in England on 16th October 1943 to provide tactical air support to the ground forces that were soon to land in France. During the following six months, the strength of the 9th was built up with the Republic Thunderbolt becoming its main fighter type. One fighter group of the 9th, the 366th, assembled at Membury after crossing from America. The three squadrons, 389th, 390th and 391st, flew their Thunderbolts from Membury in a working up capacity before moving to Thruxton. Their departure allowed the 436th Troop Carrier Group to move in from Bottesford on 3rd March 1944.

Under the command of Colonel Adriel N. Williams, the 436th was formed in 1943 in the USA and was made up of sheet metal workers, motor mechanics and many more trades. Consisting of the 79th, 80th, 81st and 82nd Troop Carrier Squadrons, the group flew the C-47 to be used in conjunction with the airborne forces. Many of the aircraft were flown directly to Bottesford whilst the

Crest of the 436th Troop Carrier Group, Membury. (C Samson)

majority of the men were transported by the *Queen Mary* to Liverpool and thence to Bottesford. Training began immediately in parachute dropping and glider towing by day and by night. The 436th then participated in four major airborne operations before renewing a period of intense training, this being carried out incorporating the 101st Airborne, known to all as the 'Screaming Eagles'! Although still a secret, the training was in preparation for D-Day. On the eve of the greatest invasion of the war, Air Marshal Sir Trafford Leigh-Mallory visited Membury and spoke words of encouragement to all the men participating in the assault.

Postponed for 24 hours, the invasion went ahead in the early hours of 6th June. With Membury a hive of activity and the entire area reverberating to the sound of the Pratt and Whitney engines

Sir Trafford Leigh-Mallory, General Eisenhower's Air Commander for D-Day, addressing men of the 436th TCG from the Membury control tower (his hands on the rail), 4th June 1944. (Ian McLoughlin)

of the C-47s, the first operation was 'Albany', the Normandy airlift, which involved 90 aircraft carrying 1,084 paratroops of the US 101st Airborne Division. They were dropped in and around the Normandy town of Ste Mere-Eglise, but 'Albany' was only partially successful, as many of the troops were dropped off the target. The 436th were later tasked in the second glider airlift for the 82nd Airborne, using two Hadrians and 48 Horsas to carry the 377th Parachute Field Artillery Regiment. The Allied forces were well and truly ashore and pushing hard inland.

History records the success of Operation Overlord and for its good work over the 6th and 7th of June, the 436th received a Distinguished Unit Citation. D-Day was an operation which was led by three airborne divisions, followed by five assault divisions with tanks landing on the beaches, followed by six more divisions with 21 more waiting in England. They were carried by 4,262 aircraft and 4,266 ships of all kinds and supported by 2,300 combat aircraft which flew 14,600 sorties on D-Day alone. In all

Airborne troops practise for the invasion – such scenes became commonplace during 1943 and 1944. (SE Newspapers)

Planes and gliders lined up at Membury ready for take-off – XVIII Corps,

14th November 1944. (Signal Corps)

of this, Membury had played a crucial part. With the Allied armies advancing quickly into France, the 436th continued the airlift of supplies, joined on D-Day+1 by the aircraft of the 442nd TCG.

With 'Overlord' over, thoughts turned to the next phase in the push to victory. During July, a detachment of C-47s from the 436th TCG flew to Italy to take part in Operation Anvil, the amphibious invasion of southern France. It was however the next operation, 'Market Garden' that prompted further men to be shipped over from the USA to join the 436th TCG at Membury.

The film *A Bridge Too Far*, which depicted the story of the operation, has become a movie classic. Sticking roughly to the true story of what happened, it tells the tale of blunder and tragedy. Like the Normandy operation that preceded it, it is now part of British and American history that is debated still today. Although the Allies had made headway into France from the Normandy invasion, they were unable to push on through Holland into Germany. The appalling weather and the fact that fuel and ammunition for the advancing Allies had to come through Normandy were holding up the speed at which the advance could continue.

The plan for 'Market Garden' was for the British 1st Airborne to take the bridges over the Neder Rijn at Arnhem, establish a bridgehead around the town and await reinforcements by the Polish 1st Parachute Brigade and the British 52nd (Airportable) Division. The US 101st were to capture the bridges over the Wilhelmina Canal, the Dommen and the Willems Canal. The US 82nd had the task of taking the Grave Bridge over the Maas and the bridge over the Waal at Nijmegen. The experience of transporting troops and towing gliders over the D-Day period had shown the full potential of this type of operation. Thus, Membury and many other bases braced themselves for another hectic period.

As 17th September 1944 approached, a cloak of security was thrown around Membury. As we have seen at the beginning of the chapter, 'Market Garden' was not the success that D-Day proved. For Membury, the two flights of 45 C-47s met far more intense flak than during the Normandy landings. During the dropping of the paratroops of the 101st, five aircraft were lost with a further 13 damaged during the first sortie. For the second drop, 11 aircraft were damaged. The following day, the C-47s and the gliders were airborne again over Holland, this time losing one with two further aircraft crash-landing back at Membury. On the third day, bad weather seriously disrupted the tows, but the sorties that were flown incurred several losses of aircraft. On 20th September, 80 C-47s dropped supplies to the troops below whilst on the 23rd, 46 aircraft towed 46 gliders to the battle area with reinforcements. By the evening of the 23rd, no further sorties were flown in support of the landings and Membury once again became a little quieter.

The winter of 1944/5 saw the 436th transporting further supplies to the Continent and carrying on the ever important training and exercises. As the new year of 1945 dawned, an air of expectancy pervaded the entire base. On 1st January, the Luftwaffe employed over 800 aircraft to attack Allied airfields in France, Belgium and Holland. It proved a disaster for the enemy and was the last major attack by the Luftwaffe. Despite this resurgence, everyone knew that time for the enemy was running out. By February, the British and Canadians had broken through the Siegfried Line and had reached the Rhine. Although the 436th had carried out supply drops over this period, the time had come for the unit to move into France and nearer the action. Between the 21st and 25th February 1945, they moved onto the Continent to be based at Melun (A-55). The 436th TCG finally returned to the United States in August 1945 and were later in-activated.

As the Americans left, Membury was handed back to the RAF. Planned to be ready for 1st July and to be taken over by No 47 Group, Transport Command, it was not until the 15th of the month that the Dakotas of No 525 Squadron moved in from nearby Lyneham. They were joined by No 187 squadron from Merryfield in October. Also flying Dakotas, both squadrons were tasked with carrying troops to the Far East. This continued for a year but with the advent of larger four-engined aircraft, the Dakotas were reduced to continental mail and newspaper deliveries. This continued until October 1946 when they moved to new locations and Membury was placed under Care and Maintenance, parented by Welford.

The base was considered as a Strategic Air Command airfield

but with various problems arising, Greenham Common was chosen instead. A resurgence of use came in 1966 when the Campbell Aircraft Company of Hungerford used Membury for flight testing their gyrocopters. Testing and production continued until the company closed down in 1976.

Today, part of the airfield is the M4 motorway, complete with a service station. Many of the buildings remain, now used by light industry whilst the T2 hangars are used for storing grain and hay. One of the local companies uses the control tower as an office and has placed plaques in memory of both American and British servicemen who had served at Membury around the walls, a fitting tribute indeed. On the 54th anniversary of 'Market Garden', 17th September 1998, a unique gathering of veterans and American and British serving personnel took place. Connected to the opening of the new Jacquet Weston Plant Ltd on the airfield site, it rekindled many memories of those troop-carrying days of 1944/5. Let us hope that Membury remains as well preserved as it is in 2000.

9

NORTHOLT

It was to a windswept Northolt that the body of Diana, Princess of Wales was returned after the tragic car accident in Paris in 1997. Now the present home of the Royal Flight, it was a fitting tribute that her coffin should be borne by the RAF upon her return to English soil. The airfield is no newcomer to royalty for being the closest military airfield to London, it is frequently used by members of the Royal household. Its other claim to fame, however, is that it is one of the earliest military airfields to have been built in the country.

Lying 14 miles to the west of London, construction had begun in 1912 with the official opening of the airfield in March 1915 when No 4 Reserve Aeroplane Squadron arrived from Farnborough. A total of 283 acres had been acquired and with the construction of six flight sheds and a single twin hangar, the site was designated a Home Defence night landing ground. Bad weather showed up a drainage problem, but this was partially cured by the laying of an area of clinker in the centre of the landing area.

It fell to No 18 Squadron of the Royal Flying Corps to christen Northolt when they formed at the base from a nucleus of No 4 Reserve Air Squadron. On 11th May 1915, equipped with Martinsyde S1s, a Shorthorn and a Bristol Scout, they began training before moving to Mousehold Heath prior to crossing the

Channel to France. Several other units used Northolt for short periods, but the next phase of its expansion came when the Fairey Aviation Company began to use the airfield for its test flying. This arrangement lasted until 1929 with flying training and test flying happily abiding side by side. With the signing of the armistice in 1918, Northolt reverted to the status of a training depot station, but with the rapid rundown in squadrons to peacetime and the closure of many airfields, Northolt became a survivor.

In being just this, civilian use of the airfield began to increase. The Central Aircraft Company was formed to carry out aerial photography and charter work, and the number of private aircraft using the facilities was on the increase. All of this convinced the military that the future of the site looked bright and a further limited period of expansion to the landing area took place. Work began on constructing more permanent buildings as the peace that had looked so full of promise in 1918 became a little tarnished.

Even this period had its inflationary problems as the Central Aircraft Company became an early victim and the business finally closed in 1926. Military activity however was on the increase as No 12 Light Bombing Squadron reformed at Northolt on 1st April 1923 with the DH9A. They were joined at the same time by No 41 who also reformed at Northolt with the Sopwith Snipe. Whilst the former moved on to Andover within the month, No 41 moved through a variety of aircraft until they were sent to Aden in 1935. Prior to their departure however, 1925 saw the formation of a number of RAF auxiliary squadrons.

Although everyone had high expectations of the peace that presently prevailed, there were obvious signs in Germany that could not be ignored. Luckily for Great Britain, some far sighted military men saw the dangers and so began an expansion of the squadrons which since the 1918 armistice had been sadly depleted.

Two auxiliary squadrons, Nos 600 (City of London) and 601 (County of London) were formed at Northolt on 14th October 1925 as light bomber squadrons. Both flew DH9s and Avro 504s. It is fair to say that 601 Squadron soon became known as the 'Millionaires Mob' since within its ranks were indeed, several

Pilots of 601 (County of London) Squadron at Northolt – the squadron eventually destroyed more than 100 enemy aircraft during the battle.

millionaires. This came about due to the original personnel being recruited from Whites Club in London, a very exclusive abode for men where Lord Edward Grosvenor handpicked his officers from his own position as commanding officer. They commenced weekend flying which included the occasional air display and participation in air exercises. Both squadrons remained at Northolt until 18th January 1927 when they moved over to nearby Hendon leaving No 41 Squadron, now equipped with the superior Bristol Bulldog, as the sole resident unit.

On 15th January 1937 the first of the many named squadrons arrived. The practice of naming RAF squadrons had its origins during the First World War, though then on a very limited scale. As the years progressed, more and more squadrons were being manned by a large proportion of Commonwealth personnel. It was also the practice of some individuals and countries to donate aircraft or give gifts of money with which to purchase aircraft. As a result of this, some squadrons had the name of a person or country incorporated in the squadron crest. Such a case was No 24 (Commonwealth) Squadron who flew their aircraft into Northolt on 15th January 1927. A communications unit, it was involved in flying Air Ministry staff and members of the Government around the country in a variety of aircraft including Avro 504s, Fairey 111Fs, DH9As and DH Moths. Its other task was to keep pilots current in flying when they were posted to administration duties at the Air Ministry.

The Bristol Bulldog was the most widely used RAF fighter until 1936. Chosen as a replacement for the Siskins and Gamecocks in RAF fighter squadrons, it had equipped No 111 Squadron since January 1931, and it was this type that they brought to Northolt on 12th July 1934. Commanded by Squadron Leader M.B. Frew, DSO, MC, AFC, the squadron were to remain at the base until just after the outbreak of the Second World War.

By this time it was becoming all too obvious that war was once again looming. As if to emphasise this fact, the death in Germany of President Hindenburg on 2nd August 1934 allowed Adolf Hitler to assume the office of both Chancellor and Fuhrer and to be sworn in as the Supreme Commander of the German Army. Around this same period, the Bulldogs of Treble One Squadron were joined by other aircraft belonging to various smaller units. They were the Air Pilotage School and the Air Fighting Development Unit, the latter to become a most valuable asset to the development of airborne radar.

With all the military activity taking place, Fairey Aviation had decided to move in July 1930 to the Great West Aerodrome, which later was to become Heathrow. In their place came a company which is still associated with military flying even today. Then a very small company designing revolutionary fighters, Martin-Baker eventually designed and built the Martin-Baker Ejection Seat, an invention to which many of today's fighter pilots owe their lives.

These early days of military expansion were not however without fatal accidents. No 24 Squadron, the communications flight, lost a DH 60M Moth on 23rd April 1931 when it crashed at Selhurst Park, Sussex, and again on 7th May lost a Fairey 111F at Wetheringham in Nottinghamshire. Treble One Squadron lost several Bulldogs and pilots in accidents whilst No 41 lost a

Hawker Demon when it crashed near Harrow. Such incidents brought home the reality that whilst flying was as safe as it could be, the unknown was always waiting to pounce.

No 24 Squadron had moved over to Hendon on 9th July 1933 with No 41 leaving for Aden on 4th October 1935. No 111 were still in residence and were joined in 1935 by the University of London Air Squadron, one of a number of units that had been suggested by Sir Hugh Trenchard many years before. At that time the idea had fallen on stony ground, but was later revived when a new Secretary of State for Air took office. Cambridge was the first to be formed followed by Oxford ten days later. By 1939 the list had risen to 100 squadrons as the halcyon days of flying continued. The London University Squadron at this time only flew on vacation periods and at annual summer camps. The units ensured a steady and regular supply of trained pilots and groundcrew for the parent service, but the outbreak of war was to see this supply dry up as a decision was made to disband all the university squadrons.

On 1st May 1936, Northolt was suddenly transferred to No 11 Group, Fighter Command with its headquarters at nearby Uxbridge. The reason for this decision very soon became all too clear.

The outbreak of the Spanish Civil War on 18th July 1936 brought the threat of a total conflict even nearer. With the news that Germany was to supply arms and technicians to aid General Franco and that two years' military service had been made compulsory in Germany, came a new realisation that peace was now at a premium. The move to place Northolt under the umbrella of Fighter Command was an indication of just how seriously the military authorities were taking the situation. Yet despite these early warnings, the RAF was not yet fully equipped for such a war.

With this realisation there now began an intense period of activity, with the aim of building an air force comparable with that of the Luftwaffe. There had already been a number of rearmament schemes, the first being drawn up and approved by the Government in July 1934 and known as Scheme A. This was intended to build an exact number of aircraft to that of the fast emerging Luftwaffe and was to be completed by 1939. A proposal for 138 squadrons, both fighter and bomber, was implemented but events in 1935 led to a hasty revision of the plan. The new one became known as Scheme C and called for an equal number of fighting machines to that of the Luftwaffe to be completed by 1937. This again was very quickly overtaken by events when on 6th March 1936, Hitler remilitarized the Rhineland and Italian aggression to its neighbours became apparent. Scheme F came into operation and again, parity with the Luftwaffe was paramount, with the addition of more use of the reserve forces together with a big airfield building programme.

The first signs at Northolt of a new expectancy began with the arrival of No 23 Squadron. Led by Squadron Leader R.J. Eccles, the Hawker Demons flew in from Biggin Hill on 21st December 1936. Some time after this, several of the aircraft were being fitted with an early form of power-operated turret made by Boulton Paul of Wolverhampton. These were not particularly successful, but the early experiments did lead to improved versions for other aircraft later on.

'A' Flight from No 111 Squadron formed the nucleus of No 213 (Ceylon) Squadron when they reformed at Northolt on 8th March 1937. They were flying another type of biplane fighter, the Gloster Gauntlet, which was in fact the fastest RAF fighter in service from 1935 to 1937. Commanded by Squadron Leader J.H. Edwards-Jones, they only stayed for a few months before moving on to Church Fenton.

That same year Group Captain A.H. Orlerar assumed command of Northolt. He arrived at a time of further increasing anxiety in the European situation. Hitler had announced to his staff in 1937 that he had a considerable programme of annexations, the first of which was the Sudetenland of Czechoslovakia. Oddly, the British and French had not at the time objected to this ambition, hoping that this particular conquest would put an end to his future ambitions. It did not for in 1938, German troops entered Austria and by 13th March, the country was declared part of Germany. All of this had its repercussions back home as the expansion continued at an even greater pace.

Northolt became one of the first airfields in the country to have two hard runways. Each was 800 yards long, one heading north-

128

east/south-west and the other north/south. A connecting perimeter track was laid, and a very elaborate camouflage system had been carried out. The airfield was preparing for war.

The prototype Hawker Hurricane had made its initial flight on 6th November 1935. A winner from the beginning, the Air Ministry immediately placed an order for 600 of the new monoplane fighter, increasing the figure to 1,000 in November 1938. It fell to Treble One Squadron at Northolt to introduce the new fighter to operations in December 1937. Conversion from the old biplane Gauntlets began immediately and was so successful that in February 1938, Squadron Leader J.W. Gillan, the squadron commander, made headline news when he made a night flight from Edinburgh to Northolt at an average speed of 408 mph with a journey time of 48 minutes. Never before had such speeds been seen.

The new aircraft, however, did bring several fatal crashes for Treble One, the first of these being on 1st February 1938. L1556 flown by Flying Officer Bocquet was practising aerobatics in the Uxbridge area when the aircraft was seen to suddenly dive directly into the ground at the junction of Western Avenue and Harefield Road. Sadly the pilot lost his life. Again on 19th March, Hurricane L1551 was forced to land on farmland at Ickenham, with a further forced landing taking place on 18th July 1938. Both pilots, however, survived.

With further signs that war was imminent, the Prime Minister Neville Chamberlain flew to meet Hitler on 22nd September 1938 at Bad Godesberg. This was his second meeting with the German Chancellor in an effort to avoid all-out war. On the previous meeting Hitler had told Chamberlain that he intended to remove all the Czechs from, and annex, Sudetenland. On 18th September, the French and British ministers met to discuss Hitler's terms and later advised the Czechs to accept. The meeting on 22nd September coincided with the resignation of the Czech Government, this in turn being followed by the Munich conference on the 29th. Having given Hitler yet again what he demanded, Prime Minister Chamberlain returned to London proclaiming, 'I believe it is peace in our time' (see Heston).

With this announcement, the tension at Northolt was relaxed a little. January 1939 began badly for 111 Squadron, however, when

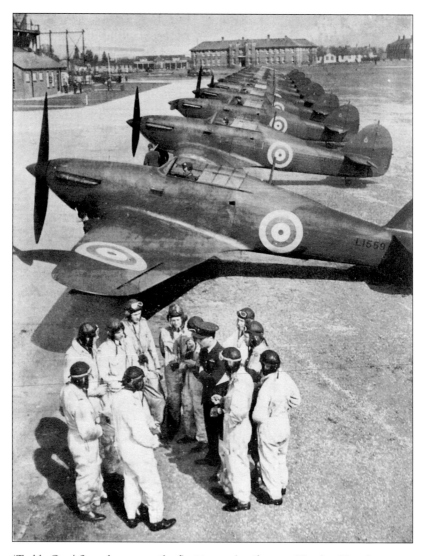

'Treble One' Squadron were the first to receive the new Hawker Hurricane. The pilots, in white flying suits, are briefed before a sortie at Northolt during 1937. (111 Squadron Archives)

In February 1940 several of 604 Squadron's Blenheims were withdrawn from service and changed to resemble German aircraft, complete with swastika. It was intended they would be flown to Finland, their disguise helping them travel unhindered, but in the end the move was abandoned. Flight Officer Selway is on the left, Flight Lieutenant John Davies on the right. (RAF Northolt)

Hurricane L1558 stalled in cloud and crashed at Alton in Hampshire. The same day L1559 crashed at Dorking, both pilots receiving severe injuries. Although for the time being, war had been averted, the work of battle formation flying and gun firing exercises continued for many weeks under the suspicion that the peace was to be shortlived.

A large C Type hangar was erected together with the usual H blocks for accommodation, this being the standard design for airfields of the period. The airfield was quickly brought up to strength with the arrival of two Blenheim squadrons. Conceived originally as a bomber, the aircraft was the result of the vast expansion scheme and represented a technical advance on the biplane Hind bomber. In 1938, with the addition of conversion kits supplied by the Southern Railways Ashford works, the Blenheim IF was conceived as a fighter with four Browning machine guns in a pack below the fuselage giving the aircraft its punch.

No 25 Squadron had converted to the Blenheim from the old biplane Gladiator and arrived at Northolt from Hawkinge on 22nd August 1939 (see *Kent Airfields in the Second World War*). Commanded by Squadron Leader D.M. Fleming, they stayed for barely a month before leaving for Filton and returning to Northolt on 4th October 1939, sending a detachment to Martlesham Heath at the same time. No 25 were joined by No 600 (City of London) auxiliary squadron, no strangers to Northolt as they had formed at the base back in 1925. They too had recently converted from the Hawker Demon to the Blenheim IF and again, like 25 Squadron, stayed only for a month before departing to Hornchurch and then to Rochford.

As further negotiations with Hitler failed during August 1939, the slide to war began to escalate. Despite recent promises, Hitler ordered attacks on Poland on 31st August. Chamberlain sent an ultimatum to Hitler that unless he was prepared to withdraw his forces from Poland, Britain would declare war on Germany. Hitler chose to ignore the cable and on 3rd September 1939, Chamberlain announced to the nation that 'Britain was therefore at war with Germany'.

By this time, Treble One Squadron were fully operational with their Hurricanes but for some unknown reason, in October 1939 they were posted north to Acklington, far from what was to become the main battle area. Their departure left Nos 25 and 600 resident at Northolt, both with the Blenheim fighter. Both squadrons now worked hard at becoming fully operational on the type, flying both day and night sorties. For 600, it was soon decreed that it was to become solely a night fighter squadron and in this role, it received the Mark IV Blenheim, equipped with the first type of airborne radar.

Although both units were now fully operational, the training continued apace as the period known as the 'Phoney War' developed. No 25 Squadron were now the sole residents, taking over the role of night fighting from 600. The flight that had been detached to Martlesham Heath began night patrols over the North Sea, and one of the first large raids behind enemy lines took place on 26th November 1939. This involved the entire

Even the ground crew liked to pose with their aircraft! The airman far left is either wearing the old style uniform or is an Air Cadet. (RAF Northolt)

squadron when, at first light on the 26th, the Blenheims left Northolt and made a long range attack on Borkum Island. Unfortunately, due to a heavy cloud layer, 25 were unable to find the target. Two days later however came success when six of the squadron aircraft together with 601 Squadron from Biggin Hill, managed to find and strafe the seaplane base.

The Phoney War continued and it appeared as though the enemy was very reluctant to fire the first shot. Heston airfield nearby had been deemed a satellite of Northolt and a dummy airfield complete with wooden aircraft and a false flarepath had been set up at a nearby golf course. As the festive season approached, Northolt personnel attempted to forget the present tension and made sure that if this was to be the last Christmas before the onslaught, it was going to be a good one.

The first Spitfires to use Northolt had arrived on 2nd October 1939 in the form of No 65 (East India) Squadron. They formed part of the Hornchurch Wing of Spitfires and had moved in from their home base. Led by Squadron Leader D. Cooke, they began a working up period in order to be ready for the inevitable battle.

November saw the first of several crashes for 25 Squadron when Blenheim L1420 crashed on landing at Northolt. With foul weather covering the entire area, a bad approach and fuel problems led to a crash landing, sadly killing the crew. Two weeks later Blenheim L1426 crashed on take-off, once again in bad weather conditions.

Christmas 1939 saw the worst snowfalls for many years. With the main water pipes freezing, it was a miserable time for all, especially for the poor army men of the 2nd Battalion, the London Scottish Regiment who were on airfield defence duties in their trenches. They were glad of the opportunity to do some snow clearing on the landing area in order just to keep warm. The engines of the Blenheims and Spitfires were run up at various intervals lest an enemy raid materialized or a night flying operation was on. At least it led to a peaceful period, the last that was to be enjoyed for many years.

The King visits an airfield defence post during a tour of Northolt. (RAF Northolt)

The new year's celebrations over, it was back to the business of war. The previous autumn had seen skirmishes with the enemy, these being mainly over the North Sea approaches, not as yet over the Channel or mainland Britain. All of this was about to change as the better weather heralded the approach of Spring.

Group Captain S.F. Vincent took command of Northolt as No 604 (County of Middlesex) auxiliary squadron arrived from nearby North Weald to relieve No 25 who had moved over to North Weald. Originally a day and night fighter unit, they were immediately reclassified as night fighters. Despite a heavy training schedule, no contact was made with the enemy until they moved down to Manston in May 1940 just ahead of Operation Dynamo. One month later No 65 Squadron returned to Hornchurch after a very dismal and disappointing time at Northolt.

Even until May, appearance of the Luftwaffe was very

6th April 1940: Sir Samuel Hoare, the Air Minister, accompanied by Air Vice Marshal Welsh, reviews 604 Squadron at Northolt. Standing smartly to attention is Flying Officer John Cunningham, later to achieve fame as a test pilot. (RAF Northolt)

spasmodic. Not so the ambitions of Hitler who on 1st March 1940, issued his invasion plans for Norway and Denmark. Hoping to forestall the invasion of the former, an Allied force sailed for Norway on 7th April. Even this could not stop the German war machine for on 1st May, the Norwegians surrendered. By the 10th, German attacks were carried out on Holland, Belgium and Luxemburg and as the army advanced towards France, the British Expeditionary Force, sent to help the French defy any German attacks, began to withdraw towards the Channel coast and Dunkirk. Operation Dynamo was about to begin.

The evacuation of the BEF began on 26th May 1940 with the entire weight of air defence falling upon Fighter Command. Goering had promised Hitler that he would prevent the Dunkirk evacuation by using his Luftwaffe, rather than the army using their tanks. Accordingly, Fliegerkorps I, II, IV and VIII were tasked to prevent it, using 300 dive-bombers and 550 fighters. Against this, Fighter Command had 600 modern fighters consisting of Hurricanes, Spitfires and Defiants. Prior to the evacuation period, No 600 (City of London) Squadron had returned with its Blenheims together with the Spitfire Is of 92 (East India) Squadron, the unit bearing the same name as No 65. Both units were based at Northolt for the evacuation period.

As Dynamo swung into action, No 609 (West Riding) auxiliary squadron, with their motto of 'Tally Ho', brought their Spitfires down from Drem in Scotland on 20th May 1940. Led by Squadron Leader M.T. Avent, they felt they had one up on many squadrons, having shot down a He 111 in February which was attacking a convoy in the North Sea. It was their first victory. They mounted their first patrol over Dunkirk on 30th May and were witness to the intense evacuation going on below them. The beleaguered army appeared as a swarm of ants as they waded out to the waiting ships. During this patrol, the Luftwaffe did not put in an appearance, but the ground barrage from the German guns just outside Dunkirk was pure hell for the soldiers waiting on the beach. Although no contact was made with the enemy, bad weather caused some of the squadron to become lost resulting in some forced landings and sadly, the death of Flight Lieutenant D. Ayres who crashed when he ran out of fuel.

No 92 (East India) Squadron flew from Northolt during the summer of 1940. (MAP)

Throughout the Dunkirk evacuation, the weather was to prove a problem. This was further amplified by the pall of dense, black smoke that hung over the entire area, the result of fiercely burning oil tanks. For the day patrols flown by 92 and 609 Squadrons it did not really prove a problem, but by night it was a different picture. Although the Blenheims had the first marks of airborne radar installed, they were not totally reliable and finding the enemy aircraft at night was not easy.

It was in fact, not until the early hours of the 10th May that 600 came into contact with the enemy. Pilot Officer Anderson on a Channel patrol came across two He 111s intent on attacking a North Sea convoy. With great skill, the observer operating the radar set brought Anderson up behind the enemy aircraft. Taking his time, the pilot lined up his quarry and fired his guns for the first time. As the roar deafened them and the smell of cordite choked them, the crew hoped to see the He 111 dive down before them. Unfortunately this was not to be, and in fact the enemy gunner managed to shoot away the hydraulics of the Blenheim. Disappointed, Anderson turned away and headed back for Manston, the nearest airfield on the Kent coast. Skilfully executing a belly landing, the crew were saved.

Two days later, six Blenheims of 600 Squadron were sent out on a daylight raid to attack German held airfields in the Low Countries. Only one aircraft returned safely. It was a grim atmosphere that pervaded all the mess areas that night at Northolt.

By 28th May, the weather over Dunkirk had deteriorated even further. Despite this, frequent patrols were mounted by the Northolt squadrons until the end of the month. By the 31st, most of the troops had been brought back with the exception of the British rearguard who were finally taken off the beaches on 2nd June. The following day the RAF gave cover to the last of the French troops embarking and by 2.23 am on the 4th June 1940, the Admiralty was able to report that Dynamo had ended: 224,585 British and 112,546 French and Belgians had been rescued from beneath the nose of the enemy. For their part, No 609 had lost five pilots and aircraft for downing three He 111s, two Bf 109s, one Do 17 and a Bf 110 claimed as destroyed.

The cost had been great for the Northolt squadrons and the RAF as a whole, but far more devastating for the Luftwaffe. Even a German radio announcer remarked, 'We must admit that the British fighters were magnificent.' Added to this, the new Prime Minister, Winston Churchill stated, 'Our air force decisively defeated the main strength of the enemy air force.' He further went on, 'Wars are not won by evacuations. But there was a victory inside this deliverance which should be noted. It was gained by the Royal Air Force.'

With Dunkirk over, life became less frantic at Northolt. The station was now a sector or controlling station in Sector Z and with the BEF safely back and nothing between the German war machine and the French Channel Ports, the country braced itself for the battle to come.

On 18th June, the remnants of No 1 Squadron began to arrive after a hasty evacuation from France. Having refuelled at Tangmere, they landed at Northolt to find what was left of their groundcrews waiting to welcome them. Their Hurricanes were in a sorry state and had to be replaced with new ones, the squadron then beginning a period of intense training with the new personnel. A detachment was sent to Hawkinge in Kent, the

A mishap to a 609 Squadron Spitfire at Northolt in June 1940. W3238
appeared to have hit a rut in the grass. (RAF Northolt)

nearest airfield to the enemy coast. The 23rd of June saw them
depart to Tangmere for a period before returning to Northolt on
1st August.

In between this period, 609 Squadron had departed to Middle
Wallop on 5th July 1940 to be replaced by No 257 (Burma)
Squadron who flew their Hurricanes in from Hendon. They soon
settled into the accommodation recently vacated by 609 and
celebrated their arrival at Northolt by shooting down a Do 17
during an early patrol. By this time the Luftwaffe were attacking
Channel convoys and with the operational area for 257 over the
Channel, contact with the enemy became frequent as the record
for Friday, 12th July 1940 shows.

Early morning mist hampered early attempts by the Luftwaffe
to attack British shipping in the Channel but with a slow burn off
as the sun rose, the first of several raids got underway by mid-

morning. Two convoys code-named 'Agent and Boots' were making their way in the Channel when a heavy attack developed over them. No 257 Squadron were held back as squadrons from No 12 Group were scrambled to intercept the raiders. A short time later it was the turn of 257 as Squadron Leader T. Harkness led his aircraft to a point mid-channel between Britain and France. By this time the convoy had moved out into the North Sea and no contact was made with the enemy. Unfortunately, two Hurricanes, L2101 and P3707, were damaged landing back at Northolt but were repairable. Both pilots were unhurt.

No 92 Squadron had left for Hornchurch on 9th June after an unsuccessful stay. Early July saw Northolt with a detachment of No 43 (China-British) arriving from Tangmere. Flying Hurricanes, they stayed for eight days before returning to Tangmere. The month carried on in similar vein with further German attacks on Channel convoys but also with a new target added, that of the coastal towns of Kent. The 19th July saw a large raid on Dover with some activity over the Isle of Wight. The radar stations warned all day of big enemy formations over the Pas-de-Calais. Fighter Command was more heavily committed than ever before, flying 701 sorties.

Total losses for the day were eight aircraft, one of them being a Hurricane, P3471, of No 1 Squadron. Pilot Officer D.O.M. Browne was forced to land in flames outside Brighton after his aircraft was hit in the glycol tank by return fire from a He 111 of KG55. Not to be outdone, red section of No 1 attacked another He 111. Inflicting damage on the bomber, it was eventually shot down by 145 Squadron with Uffz Biskup, FW Maeder and Oblt Westhaus killed and FW Kaster and Gefr Mensel missing. Earlier in the day, No 257 Squadron had attacked one of the Dorniers bombing Dover. Although this aircraft had been attacked first by 145 Squadron from Tangmere, it fell to the crew of a squadron Blenheim – Flying Officer Mitchell, Pilot Officer Bon Seigneur and Sergeant Hulbert – to finish it off. They had the satisfaction of seeing it drop into the Channel.

The rest of July saw similar operations. Not being directly in the front line, ie Kent and Sussex, the Northolt squadrons did not see as much action as their comrades. None the less, they had their moments of glory and of despair.

Sunday, 28th July dawned fine and warm. The enemy on this day confined most of their attacks to the Channel and East Coast. At 2 pm, more than a hundred enemy aircraft were plotted crossing the Channel. No 257 were scrambled in time and met the enemy mid-Channel. Together with 74, 41 and past Northolt residents, 111 Squadrons, they harrassed the formation, shooting down two of the bombers. Hurricane P3622 of 257 flown by Sergeant R.V. Forward was seriously damaged in the dogfights with Bf 109s of JG26 and was forced to land at Hawkinge. Whilst he was luckily unhurt, his aircraft was a write-off.

As the month came to an end, it was declared that for all their efforts, the Luftwaffe had only sunk 18 small steamers and four destroyers. Whilst they had also shot down 145 British fighters, they themselves had lost 270 aircraft. It was however, not the loss of aircraft that worried Air Chief Marshal Hugh Dowding, the chief of Fighter Command, but the shortage of pilots. The lost aircraft were being replaced within a week's output from the factories, but the training of a pilot took considerably longer. With high summer fast approaching, both he and his commanders knew that the ferocity of the air battles could only increase with mainland Britain itself becoming the main target.

On 1st August 1940, Hitler issued directive No 17 to his military. In it he instructed the Luftwaffe to overpower the British Air Force in the shortest possible time. The attacks were to be carried out against flying units, ground installations and manufacturing plants. The real Battle of Britain was about to begin.

With the rapid advances of the German Army into Poland during 1939, many Poles had fled the country ahead of the German invasion. Many came to the UK and included in this category were Polish Air Force personnel whose one ambition was to hit back at the enemy that had overrun their country. Thus the formation of several Polish squadrons took place, the first being No 302 (Poznan) Squadron which formed at Leconfield on 13th July 1940. The second unit, No 303 (Kosciusko) formed at Northolt on 2nd August under a British CO, Squadron Leader R.G. Kellett. Thirteen Polish Officer pilots, eight Polish NCOs and 135 Polish ground staff arrived to join the skeleton British personnel who had been getting ready for their arrival. Though the pilots could already fly military aircraft, the Hurricane was very unfamiliar with its retractable undercarriage and eight guns. They did however learn very quickly and actually beat No 302 in reaching operational efficiency. It was the lack of the English language that was to prove harder to overcome.

Crash courses were held at Northolt in basic English coupled with flying tuition on one Miles Magister, a Fairey Battle light bomber and eight Hurricanes. The CO and two Flight Commanders, Flight Lieutenants Atholl Forbes and Johnny Kent were duplicated by Polish personnel, these being Squadron Leader Krasnodemski and Flight Lieutenants Henneberg and Lapkowski. Whilst some considerable progress was made in basic English, in the air the excitement seemed to take over and they reverted to their native tongue. This prompted the CO or either of the Flight Commanders to shout obscenities over the intercom in English to bring them back into line. Sometimes it even managed to work! No 303 were eventually deemed ready for battle by 24th August, the height of the Battle.

Early August, however, gave way to warm weather with

Flight Sergeant Wadaw Giermer and Sergeant Barderczik reflect on the spoils of war, a Luftwaffe Iron Cross. (RAF Northolt)

temperatures above average. Though the attacks on British convoys in the Channel continued, more and more the enemy aircraft were crossing to raid coastal towns. The return of No 1 Squadron on 1st August heralded an intense time at Northolt. With their Hurricanes joining those of No 257, the station entered a very busy period. No 1 sent detachments to Tangmere, Manston, North Weald and Heathrow during their stay and although these detachments had some contact with the enemy, it was not until the 11th of the month that No 1 tangled with the Luftwaffe.

It was a Sunday and although the early morning broke fine, the cloud soon thickened giving a heavy covering by mid-morning. From 7 in the morning to around 10.30 pm, a series of probing raids by the enemy had developed against Dover. Several formations then attacked the Dover Balloon Barrage and 15 minutes later a force of 30+ aircraft approached the English coast in an effort to draw the RAF into battle. Though unknown at this

Pilots of No 1 Squadron: l to r – Drake, Clisby, Lorimer, Hanks, Mould, Squadron Leader Halahan, Moses, Demozay, Walker, Doc Brown, Richey, Kilmartin, Mitchell and Palmer. (No 1 Sqn Archives)

time, the idea was to attract as many fighters as possible to the Dover area whilst the main bomber force hit Portland naval base in Dorset.

No 1 were scrambled from Northolt as the plots came into the sector operations room thick and fast. Vectored to an area above the Isle of Wight, they entered the fray. Together with 17 Squadron from Debden and 64 from Kenley, they ensured that the enemy formation was soon in disarray. Setting his sights on a Bf 110, Pilot Officer J.A.J. Davey in Hurricane P3172 went into the attack. The German pilot however returned the fire, hitting the Hurricane which immediately began to emit smoke as it entered a steep dive. It crashed on Sandown Golf Course at 11.20 am, sadly killing Davey. In the same action, the Hurricane of Pilot Officer R.H. Shaw was forced to crashland at Tangmere without loss of life. Minutes later No 1 avenged the death of Pilot Officer Davey when they sent a Bf 110 into the Channel before returning to Northolt. Whilst the afternoon was quiet, at the end of the day the battle honours were fairly even with 38 German aircraft shot down together with 32 British.

The next day it was the turn of 257 to suffer at the hands of the enemy. On a day forever known as the 'Glorious 12th' in the grouse hunting fraternity, likewise for the Luftwaffe it was to be the 'glorious 12th' though for a very different reason. This was the day devoted to the first of many attacks on British airfields. Two large German units, Luftflotten 2 and 3, were delegated for these opening attacks, divided into five phases devoted to hitting coastal airfields, radar stations and continued attacks on shipping and harbours.

The first attacks came shortly after 7 am when the Bf 110s of Erprobungs Gruppe 210 led by Hauptmann Walter Rubensdoerffer attacked the coastal radar towers. First Dunkirk near Canterbury, then Pevensey, followed by Rye and Dover. At Dunkirk, the 110s bombed with deadly accuracy as two huts received direct hits and a 1,000lb bomb landed near the transmitting tower. Despite this damage, it continued to operate. The same happened at Dover as telephone cables were severed and all communication with Stanmore, the plotting station, was cut for several hours. Their work done, the 110s returned to Calais-Marke in France to allow the next wave to come in. This consisted of Stuka Ju 87 dive-bombers who attacked convoys Agent and Arena in the Thames Estuary, whilst the Ju 88s of Luftflotte 3 with a heavy fighter escort attacked Portsmouth naval base. Fifty eight RAF fighters were scrambled to repel the attack, but still the bombers got through and hit the town and dockyard, leaving a trail of destruction.

The telephone rang at 257's dispersal at around midday. 'Squadron scramble', shouted the orderly airman. In a rush of boots and flying jackets, the pilots ran to their waiting Hurricanes. Into the cockpit, harness on, contact and taxi to the runway. By 12.10 pm they were airborne and heading for Portsmouth. They caught the bombers as they were returning to France and promptly went into the attack. Several bombers fell to the Hurricanes' guns but sadly, Pilot Officer J.A.G. Cholmley in P3662 was last seen trailing smoke as he headed toward the coast. Neither he nor his aircraft were ever found. In the same raid, Hurricane P3776 flown by Flying Officer the Hon D.A. Coke was hit by enemy fire and crash-landed in a farmer's field. The aircraft was deemed repairable, with Coke being admitted to Haslar Royal Naval Hospital.

By early evening, the German High Command were confident that all the radar stations, airfields and towns that they had attacked were out of action. Nothing was further from the truth, but this sort of exaggeration was to continue throughout the war, both in Germany and in Britain, though here to a lesser extent. All of the radar stations attacked were actually back in action within hours and most of the airfields, such as Hawkinge, Lympne and Manston, were operational by the next day. The RAF flew 500 sorties on this one day, losing 22 aircraft whilst the enemy lost 29.

'From Reichsmarschall Goering to all units of Air Fleets 2, 3 and 5. Operation Eagle. Within a short period, the RAF will be wiped from the skies. Heil Hitler.'

Adlertag or Eagle Day had arrived. The beginning of the end for the RAF. At least, so thought the Germans. As dawn broke over Northolt on 14th August, men from both the resident squadrons rose early and looked up at the brightening sky. Early morning mist hung low over the airfield and now and then a slight drizzle was felt. On the other side of the Channel, the enemy too were looking at the dawn sky. Luftlotten 2 and 3 were already geared for the great attack, and groundcrews had been busy since before first light to make sure the bombers and fighters were ready. As the plans for the attacks on the British fighter airfields began to formulate, a layer of cloud arrived over the area. This did not seem to deter the first formation from taking off, but a signal from the Reichsmarshall himself calling off the first attacks until the weather cleared went unheeded. Whilst the fighter escort heard the message, the 74 Do 17s of KG2 led by Oberst Johannes Fink had a different type of crystal in their radio sets and did not therefore receive the instructions. Thus, they carried on to bomb Eastchurch airfield in Kent.

The afternoon saw clearer skies as the real thrust of Eagle Day began. Large formations attacked the airfields and towns as Fighter Command became fully committed. No 257 were scrambled at 3 pm, losing two Hurricanes, P3601 and P3623, to return fire. Pilot Officer C.F.A. Capon and Sergeant D.J. Hulbert were unhurt with both aircraft deemed repairable. By the evening, Eagle Day had cost the Luftwaffe 43 aircraft whilst Fighter Command had lost 14.

Thursday, 15th August became known to the Luftwaffe as *Schwarze Donnerstag*, Black Thursday. It was on this day that the enemy lost 76 aircraft, their highest loss on any day during the Battle. For Northolt it also became a black day when No 1 lost two pilots and three Hurricanes.

Scrambled at 2.30 pm, the nine Hurricanes climbed to 1,500 feet to intercept a raid approaching the East Coast. Sighting the enemy, Squadron Leader Brown noted 20 Bf 110s escorted by a similar number of Bf 109s. What he did not know was that they were from the crack Luftwaffe fighter-bomber experimental unit known as Erprobungs 210 based at Calais-Marke airfield in France. As the Hurricanes of No 1 met them head on, Flight Lieutenant M.H. Brown was immediately attacked and forced to bale out. Although burnt, he was rescued from the Channel by a trawler and taken to hospital. Not so lucky were Pilot Officer D.O.M. Browne in Hurricane R4075 and Sergeant M.M. Shanaham in Hurricane P3043. Both men were shot down over the Channel, neither their aircraft or bodies being found. Over the target, Flying Officer P. Matthews leading A section, sent one of the Bf 110s down in flames whilst Pilot Officer H.T. Mann managed to shoot the cockpit off a Bf 109. In the same dogfight, Hurricane P3678 flown by Pilot Officer J.F.D. Elkington was damaged in combat and crashlanded at Northolt, the pilot being unhurt.

That night the atmosphere at Northolt was very solemn. No one felt like celebrating their victories for the loss of three of their comrades, for it appeared as though the luck for No 1 was running out. Yet, whilst it had been a bad day for the squadron, many German units that same evening were also mourning their dead. The Luftwaffe had carried out 1,750 sorties against England from first light until darkness. The figures did not please Hitler, and Goering was immediately summoned to Berlin. Late that night, the Luftwaffe chief issued an order prohibiting the presence of more than one officer in any single aircrew in an attempt to stem the loss of senior personnel. Although not known at this time to Dowding and Fighter Command, the enemy was certainly not having it all his own way.

The next day, Friday 16th August, the aircraft losses for the squadron were as bad, though with no loss of life. They had been scrambled at midday to patrol Tangmere when they came into a minor conflict with some Bf 109s. The engagement was brief as the enemy turned back to France, but poor Pilot Officer Elkington was again a victim of return fire and was forced to bale out over Thorney Island, watching his beloved P3173 bury itself at Manor Farm, Chidham. Landing heavily at 1.05 pm, he was admitted to hospital with leg injuries.

Again in the afternoon, Squadron Leader Pemberton led 'A' Flight into the attack at 4.30 pm, followed closely by 'B' Flight. Diverted to London, a cry of 'Tally Ho' received in the Northolt Operations Room indicated that the squadron had met the enemy. Attacking the first wave of enemy aircraft from behind, No 1 avenged the previous day's losses with great ferocity. As the last of the enemy was forced to retire and head home, the squadron notched up four He 111s, one Ju 88 and a Bf 109 with two Heinkels and one Messerschmitt destroyed. All of this within the space of 40 minutes!

Back at Northolt, No 257 had by now moved over to Debden leaving No 1 and the Polish 303 Squadron as the sole residents. The day following the 16th proved to be fairly quiet as low cloud covered much of the area. Even so, No 1 were dispersed to North

Polish pilots of No 303 Squadron await a scramble at Northolt in September 1940. Most squadrons had a mascot – 303 chose a terrier. (RAF Northolt)

Weald and attacked an enemy reconnaissance flight just after 1 pm. Squadron Leader Pemberton shot down a straggler over Tenterden, but heavy cloud prevented any further action. Returning to Northolt they were again scrambled, but failed to find the enemy with the deteriorating weather conditions.

Forever known in history as 'the hardest day', Sunday 18th August was the day that the Luftwaffe finished the week-long attempt to destroy Fighter Command. The main objectives were again the fighter airfields although so far, Northolt had not been subjected to an attack. The first of the massed formations were over the coast by midday and although No 1 was scrambled on this occasion, only one Hurricane, P3757, was damaged in combat, Pilot Officer G.E. Goodman returning to Northolt with his aircraft repairable. Though most other squadrons saw many sorties on this particular day, No 1 were held back.

By nightfall, the news for the German High Command was bleak. The immense losses of Stuka Ju 87 dive-bombers ensured that the rest of the aircraft were rapidly withdrawn from the battle. The decision had come about after the Stukas of STG77, whilst attacking Poling radar station and airfields along the

148

Hampshire coast, had suffered grievously at the hands of Fighter Command – together with other aircraft types, the Luftwaffe had lost 194 aircraft from the 15th to 18th August.

Despite these losses on the 18th, the enemy formations had managed to put the Chain Home Low radar station at Poling completely out of action. Together with the Ventnor radar station which had been out of operation since the 12th August raids, it left a large gap in the early warning system. Though this was partially covered by a series of smaller mobile radar stations, for Fighter Command it was still a serious setback. Fate however took a hand, and cloudy weather from 19th to 23rd August now intervened allowing repair work on the CHL sites to carry on uninterrupted. Likewise, the lack of enemy attacks allowed Fighter Command to recoup some of its losses, and to send hard pressed fighter squadrons to quieter areas for rest and refit.

As the second phase of the battle continued, at Northolt it was time for the Polish squadron, No 303, to become fully operational. In addition, with the departure of 257 Squadron, No 1 Squadron of the Royal Canadian Air Force had arrived from Croydon. Commanded by Squadron Leader E.A. McNab, DFC, the Hurricanes had been attached to No 111 Squadron, old Northolt residents, for training purposes but on their arrival at Northolt were deemed fully operational. Scrambled on 26th August for the first time, they encountered a formation of 20+ Do 17s. In the ensuing battle, the squadron shot down three enemy aircraft with three damaged. Sadly, they also lost three Hurricanes with one pilot, Pilot Officer R.L. Edwards killed. Over the same period until 31st August, No 1 RAF also lost two aircraft with no deaths.

For 303 Polish Squadron, operational status could not come soon enough. Still commanded by Squadron Leader Kellett, their first action came on 30th August during a training flight. Prior to this, the training had included feint attacks on Blenheims. One problem with the Poles that eventually came to light was their inexperience with retractable undercarriages, something that caused a few losses in Hurricanes. In order to remedy this, Group Captain Vincent, the Northolt CO, demanded that an airman be situated at the end of the runway complete with a Verey pistol. When it was noticed that a Polish pilot was about to land with his undercarriage up, a red flare across the nose would awaken the hapless pilot.

Formating with the Blenheims for another training flight on 30th August, 'B' Flight by chance saw an enemy formation in the distance. This was like a red flag to a bull as 303 noticed the large Swastikas and Balkan Crosses. It proved too much for Flying Officer Paszkiewicz who broke formation and promptly shot down a Do 17. This of course was a perfect excuse to break into their own language with excitement over the RT, followed by a string of obscenities telling them to shut-up from the flight commander. The incident, however, proved a point and Squadron Leader Kellett was pleased to receive a signal from Fighter Command: 'As from today, 303 is operational.'

Saturday, 31st August was to see Fighter Command's heaviest losses – 39 fighters shot down with 14 pilots killed. Dowding's forces were now suffering from a mounting loss of pilots coupled with a large fatigue factor in those who managed to survive. With the raids by the enemy on the airfields showing no abatement, the question was just how long Fighter Command could sustain the onslaught before the loss of both pilots and aircraft reached the point of no return.

It was 'A' Flight of 303 who were tasked with the last scramble of the day at 18.25 hours. With six Hurricanes patrolling east of Biggin Hill at 16,000 feet, Squadron Leader Kellet saw a large formation of Do 17s escorted by Bf 109s. He led his fighters into the attack, flying in line astern and from out of the sun. They achieved complete surprise. The CO shot one down in flames whilst Sergeant S. Karubin fired on a second 109 and followed it down into a dive. When the enemy levelled out, he again attacked from 200 yards range. As the 109 dived away, Karubin gave a last three-second burst and the enemy erupted into flames. A third pilot, Sergeant E.M. Szaposznikow fired on another 109 which rolled onto its back and fell to the ground. Three other pilots sent further 109s into the sea. They were learning fast.

As September dawned and despite the fact that the enemy had so far not attacked Northolt airfield itself, the resident squadrons were feeling the effects of continuous battle. Sunday, 1st September saw Flight Sergeant F.G. Berry killed when his

Hurricane, P3276, was hit by fire from a Bf 109 over Tonbridge. Two days later during a Luftwaffe attack on Hornchurch airfields, the squadron lost Pilot Officer R.H. Shaw and Flight Lieutenant H.B.L. Hillcoat, both bodies not being recovered. In the case of the former however, it is fairly certain that it is Robert Shaw that rests in a memorial garden at Chart Sutton near Maidstone where a service is held in September each year. No positive identification has ever been forwarded by the MOD, and the cross at the head of the grave only records 'An unknown airman'.

Heavy attacks on the airfields continued for the first six days of September. Over this period, 303 Squadron lost eleven Hurricanes with no loss of life although there were injuries, with No 1 losing one aircraft with one injury.

Friday, 6th September heralded the onset of an early autumn, but it was also noticed by the country that a change in enemy tactics was becoming apparent. The day carried only three main enemy attacks and the night of the 6th/7th was less active than usual. The Fighter Controllers naturally assumed that the Luftwaffe was resting to recoup its losses but in fact, the German policy of attacking radar sites and airfields was about to change, sadly at the expense of the civilian population but luckily for Dowding and the fighter airfields.

Across the Channel at Calais-Marke airfield, a very large Mercedes car swept through the main gate. Seated in the back, the flamboyant and colourful figure of Reichsmarschall Goering was grinning and saluting his airmen at the same time. Pulling the car to a stop, he announced to them all, 'I have taken over personal command of the Luftwaffe in its war against England.' Later he moved onto the cliffs along the Pas-de-Calais just a short distance from the airfield. There, with his hands over his ears, he looked at the huge armada flying overhead and heading for England. The target this time was London and the commencement of the Blitz.

The Chain Home Low radar station at Foreness in Kent picked up the formation and passed the information on to Stanmore, where a Waaf plotter moved a marker on the large map table indicating 50+ enemy aircraft approaching the coastline. At Northolt, Nos 1 and 303 Squadrons were on stand-by and with trolley-acs plugged into the Hurricanes were awaiting the scramble. It came at 4.15 pm and five minutes later, both were airborne. It soon became obvious to the fighter controllers at the sector stations that a different scenario was opening. The enemy formations passed over the usual targets of the airfields and kept going. It was realised the sole target was now the capital.

As the bombs rained down on London, Nos 1 and 303 were told to wait for the bombers on their home run. This was a danger time for the bombers for with their fighter escort having left them due to lack of fuel, they were vulnerable to attack from the air and from the ground. With superior height and a setting sun, both squadrons tore into the retreating aircraft. Although it seemed like hours, in minutes No 1 had sent a Bf 109 and a Do 17z down in flames with no loss to themselves. Returning to Northolt, the crews could see the black pall of smoke that hung over the capital. The aircraft were immediately refuelled and rearmed, and were scrambled again at 5.50 pm, damaging two Do 17s with no loss. It was a different story for No 303 who lost four Hurricanes with no loss of life to pilots, although they did sustain injuries. Sadly, the crash of Hurricane P4173 flown by Flying Officer M. Pisarek, caused the death of three civilians when it came down on to an air raid shelter in Loughton.

The next day, with pilots and groundcrews showing severe fatigue, No 1 were posted for a rest period to Wittering. In from Wittering came No 229 Squadron, which had been in training since its rapid exit from France. The Hurricane Is arrived under the command of Squadron Leader Banham who had recently taken over from Squadron Leader H.J. Maguire. They were soon thrown into the fray with Wednesday, 11th September being a memorable first. Together with Nos 1 RCAF and 303 Polish Squadrons, they were scrambled during the afternoon in defence of a large attack on London carried out by Heinkel bombers of KG1 and KG26. Though the Canadians lost two Hurricanes and No 229 lost three, the only deaths were with No 303 who also lost two aircraft, but with Sergeant S. Wojtowicz and Flying Officer A. Cebrynski sadly losing their lives.

The scoreboard for Fighter Command on this day made depressing reading with the loss of 29 aircraft, 17 pilots killed and six wounded. The enemy had lost 25 aircraft with many deaths, KG26 being the worst hit losing eight He 111s. The lack of success by the Luftwaffe in clearing the RAF from the skies was partially hidden from Hitler and the German High Command. The plan for a seaborne invasion of England, codenamed 'Sealion', was still intended for the middle of September providing the Luftwaffe had air superiority. At the moment they did not, yet still the planned invasion was deemed possible.

The next few days were unsettled, and in the main only sporadic raids were carried out. As Sunday, 15th September 1940 dawned fair, the Luftwaffe prepared for one last gigantic thrust in order to bring the RAF and the civilian population to its knees. Now celebrated annually as Battle of Britain Day, it failed in its purpose, but it was a day of ferocious fighting.

With the barometer rising high, the enemy reconnaissance aircraft were out early, forewarning the radar stations of the big raids to come. By 11 pm, the sky over the Pas-de-Calais was black with aircraft as they formed up into armadas to cross the Channel. All the 11 Group airfields were at readiness together with No 12 and 13 Groups. At 11.15 pm, the Northolt squadrons were climbing to a patrol area between 1,500 and 25,000 feet. The battle raged hard and long with the skies above London and Kent streamed with aircraft contrails.

Three Hurricanes of No 1 RCAF were shot down early in the battle with Flying Officer R. Smither sadly killed. No 229 were to lose two aircraft and one pilot, but worst of all 303 lost eight aircraft with one pilot lost, Sergeant M. Brzezowski, who was presumed drowned when his Hurricane was seen to crash into the Thames Estuary. In the same dogfight, the CO, Squadron Leader Kellett, was damaged in combat but returned safely to Northolt, his aircraft repairable. Group Captain Vincent, the station CO, had taken a spare Hurricane into the battle and had confronted eight Do 17s who, when he flew into the midst of them, broke away and turned for home with no stomach for a fight.

The Prime Minister, Winston Churchill, had been at Bentley Priory with the commander of 11 Group, Air Vice-Marshal Keith Park on this day. He recalled, 'I had watched in silence until I said, what other reserves have we?' 'There are none,' said Park. Churchill again recalled, 'It indeed looked grave.'

Such was the situation on that fateful day. Even a detachment of the much maligned Boulton Paul Defiants from No 264 (Madras Presidency) Squadron were airborne from Northolt on 15th September, though perhaps luckily after previous failures of the aircraft in battle, did not come into contact with the enemy. By nightfall the South East was littered with the wrecks of enemy aircraft. For the Germans it had been a disaster and this was the deciding factor in the German High Command changing from daylight bombing to that of night. Never again were such vast numbers of enemy aircraft to be seen in daylight.

Although not directly associated with the change in enemy tactics, Northolt became subject to a succession of visitors. Being the only 11 Group airfield that had not been battered by the past few months, it had kept its buildings intact and was therefore not the shambles that others looked. The Canadian squadron were to receive their ambassador and the Canadian press, whilst His Majesty King George VI toured the station and visited all the squadron dispersals. During his inspection a raid developed over Portsmouth and Group Captain Vincent invited His Majesty

General Sikorski decorates Wing Commander Kolski, Squadron Leader Janusiewici, and Flight Lieutenant Kotocskiocoski at Northolt, 1940. (RAF Northolt)

to listen in at the newly commandeered Z Sector operations room in Ruislip as the Northolt squadrons were scrambled. The King was later informed that up until that time the squadrons had claimed 148 aircraft destroyed, 22 probables and 52 damaged, a very satisfying score.

Three months less ten days had now gone by since the start of the Battle of Britain. Germany had not succeeded in clearing the RAF from the skies, and there was very little to set against the loss of 1,653 aircraft. By coincidence, 30th September was the day that the King appointed Hugh Dowding a Knight Grand Commander of the Bath. With hindsight and on reflection of how this great commander was to be treated later on by his peers, it was none too soon.

The remainder of the month saw the fighting continue though on a reduced scale. Despite this, all three Northolt squadrons lost aircraft and pilots with the last day of the month proving difficult for 229 Squadron. With two major raids beginning by 9 am, 229 met the second wave over Kent and in the space of minutes had lost eight aircraft, though with just one death, that of Flying Officer M. Ravenhill who was shot down by a Bf 109 and crashed at Church Road, Ightham. It was a bad end to the month for 229.

The fourth phase of the battle entered a new dimension, that of the fighter/bomber flying at high altitude to escape detection and confrontation, the bomber being reserved for night bombing. Sunday, 4th October was a significant day in the history of the station when it was attacked for the first time. It fell to a Ju 88 of KG30 under the command of Oberst Loedel to cause death and destruction. Taking off from Aalborg in Denmark at around 1 pm, the formation broke into smaller units, some of which attacked Middle Wallop in Hampshire and one aircraft in particular, Northolt. It is widely believed that this aircraft, a Ju 88A-1, was coded 4D-DT and carried the crew of Gefr Boebel, Oberfw Ortlepp, Uffz Roeder and Uffz Holmeier.

Running in from the southern perimeter at around 200 feet, it began machine-gunning some buildings. As it passed over the large C Type hangar, it dropped two bombs which landed in between that and another hangar. With one gigantic explosion the ground erupted, with earth and flame being thrown a considerable distance. Having no prior warning of the attack,

The aftermath of the October 1940 raid; Sergeant Antoni Suidak's Hurricane P3120 totally wrecked by the raid. (Polish Institute)

most personnel did not have time to take cover yet only two were killed. One was Sergeant Antoni Suidak who was caught taxiing in his Hurricane, and the other was the airman on look-out duty, AC2 H.E. Stennet. One other Hurricane was also damaged. After it had dropped its bombs, the Ju 88 continued its machine-gunning until escaping into cloud. No 229 had two Hurricanes airborne at the time who did manage to register some hits on the enemy until it disappeared. The aircraft in question, however, later crashed in Surrey with Gefr Boedel being killed and the other three members missing. Back at Northolt, most of the station personnel were put to removing the remains of the aircraft and filling in the large craters so by the next day, operations could continue as usual.

Having re-equipped with Spitfires in October 1940, No 615 Squadron moved to Northolt to continue the fight in late October. (RAF Northolt)

It was now time for No 1, the Canadian squadron to be sent to a quieter area and on 9th October, they left for Prestwick in Scotland. Not sorry to go for they had seen some of the heaviest fighting in the sector, they were replaced by No 615 (County of Surrey) auxiliary squadron who flew their Hurricanes in under the command of Squadron Leader J.R. Kayll, DSO, DFC. They had received a rough time whilst based at Kenley in Surrey, and had been sent to Prestwick to rest. They now came to Northolt to take on offensive operations over the Channel as well as scrambling to intercept the few large raids that were still coming over by day.

The day after their arrival, it was the turn of No 303 to move to a quieter area as they departed to Leconfield. The squadron had found great success whilst at Northolt and although they still mourned their losses, the one Czech pilot in the squadron, Sergeant Josef Frantisek, had achieved the highest score of any Allied pilot during September, that of 17 aircraft destroyed. Sadly and for no apparent reason, whilst he was flying Hurricane R4175 the day before the squadron left for Leconfield, his aircraft

615 Squadron land at Northolt after a sortie during the Battle of Britain.
(RAF Northolt)

dropped from the sky during a routine patrol over Surrey and he was killed. A sad and tragic loss. No 302 (Poznan) Polish Squadron, which was the first Polish squadron to be formed, arrived in their place. They were soon continuing the good work carried out by their comrades but on a relatively quiet day for attacks, they were to suffer grievously at the hands of the weather.

It was Friday, 18th October, with fog in the Straits of Dover and the Thames Estuary which persisted all day though thinning at times. The previous night had been busy but the morning, due to the fog, was very quiet. Forty five standing RAF patrols were flown including one by 302 from Northolt. Getting airborne at around 3.45 pm, the weather deteriorated so rapidly that it became the cause of four deaths. Pilot Officers S. Wadniarek, A. Zukowski, P.E.G. Carter and Flying Officer J. Borowski were all killed when they crashed in fog. Another Hurricane of 302 was forced to crashland, Pilot Officer B. Bernas surviving unhurt. It had been a dreadful day for the Poles and one that once again brought a feeling of despair and grief to Northolt.

Between this time and the end of the month, 302 Squadron lost Flight Lieutenant F. Jastrzebski when he failed to return from patrol. No 229 lost Pilot Officer D.B.H. McHardy who was believed captured when he was shot down over the French coast during an attack on a He 59, a large floatplane used for air-sea rescue work. By the end of the month with bad weather settling in, it was deemed that the Battle of Britain had reached its end. Operation Sealion had been cancelled temporarily until the spring brought better weather and the vast attacks upon the fighter airfields had all but finished. It was the blitz and hit-and-run raids that were now coming to the fore.

November saw Nos 229, 302 and 615 Squadrons still at Northolt. The station had remained operational throughout the battle with the October score standing at 22 destroyed, 3 probables and 15 damaged. December was a time of change as 302 left for Westhampnett in Sussex (see *Sussex Airfields in the Second World War*) and later in the month, both 229 and 615 left, the former to Wittering whilst 615 moved back to Kenley.

A pilot of 615 Squadron poses by his Spitfire whilst a member of the ground crew plugs in the trolley acc for starting the aircraft. (RAF Northolt)

615 Squadron at Northolt, October 1940 – there appear to be two French pilots on the far left. (RAF Northolt)

No 601 (County of London) auxiliary squadron, the 'Millionaires Mob', returned on 17th December to their old haunt. Being well within the reach of all the London clubs, they were glad to be back although at this point, morale in the squadron appeared very low. Three months of inactivity whilst being rested at Exeter and a dramatic change in personnel all added to the general feeling. Equipped with Hurricanes, the CO, Squadron Leader J.A. O'Neill, DFC, had recently taken over from Squadron Leader Sir A.P. Hope and it was his task to get morale up and bind the squadron into its original fighting form. Back also came No 1 Squadron though this time only until the new year.

The advent of the year saw Fighter Command begin its long offensive against the Luftwaffe on 10th January 1941. The new initiative had a language of its own. Circus, Rhubarb, Rodeo, Ranger and Roadstead were all names for a variety of offensive operations.

As the blitz of London continued by night and less by day,

many bombs fell within the vicinity of Northolt though not directly on the station. No 303 (Kosciusko) Polish Squadron returned for another stay, this time of some duration. Shortly after they arrived they exchanged their ageing Hurricanes for the Spitfire Mk.I. Though these were considered an improvement, they were no match for the new variants of Me 109s that were being used by the Luftwaffe for their high altitude work. (By 1941 the Bf 109 was more commonly called the Me 109 plus the variant number.) The 'F' variant for this high altitude work had begun to appear in November 1940 and clearly had an advantage over the Hurricane and the early marks of Spitfire. The Air Staff were fully aware of this and to counter this new threat, more powerful Merlin engines were being fitted to the new marks of Spitfire. No 303 now took the offensive flying fighter sweeps over the Channel, codenamed 'Rodeos'.

No 1 Squadron had finished 1940 without incident on their return to Northolt and on New Year's Eve, Flight Lieutenant

No 1 Squadron re-equipped with the cannon-firing Hurricane IIc in August 1941 shortly after leaving Northolt – this fine picture shows them in flight. (Aeroplane)

161

Clowes was briefed for a special operation the next day. Together with two other pilots, Pilot Officers Lewis and Kershaw, the plan was for them to undertake the first offensive operation for the squadron, that of attacking German installations along the Pas-de-Calais. Though the cloud cover was thick, the mission was a success and gave the enemy a taste of what he could now expect from an air force on the offensive. No 1 moved to Kenley on 4th January 1941 to continue this work.

Now 303 and 601 Squadrons were partnered at Northolt for many months to come. They carried out many fighter sweeps over enemy territory, shooting at targets of opportunity. On other occasions they flew Rhubarbs, low level strike operations, and Ramrods, when both squadrons escorted bombers on daylight raids over occupied Europe. This was the pattern of operations from Northolt for at least half the year. 601 Squadron converted to the Hurricane IIB in March whilst at the base. This new mark of Hurricane introduced an armament of twelve .303 machine guns, packing a larger punch than the Mk.I. These delivered an even more devastating firepower on ground targets, and 601 were to use them to good effect. On 1st May they moved down to Manston on the Thanet coast, and did not return to Northolt.

By this time all of the Polish Squadrons, Nos 302 to 309, were equipped with various marks of Spitfire and in April, 303 were joined by No 306 (Torun) Polish Squadron. The 24th June 1941 saw No 308 (Krakow), another Polish squadron arrive from Chilbolton, to be joined at Northolt on 14th July 1941 by 315 (Deblin) Polish Squadron. The arrival of the new squadrons coincided with a change of command at Northolt when Group CaptainVincent was posted elsewhere. He had seen the station through its most difficult period and had shared in the triumphs and losses of all the squadrons that had served there through the Battle of Britain. With a sad heart he left for his new appointment, to be replaced by Group Captain McEvoy.

The four Polish squadrons now roamed far and wide over enemy territory. In April the satellite airfield at Heston gained squadron status with two of the squadrons from Northolt using it as their permanent base. They all rotated through a variety of marks of Spitfire, one of the most devastating being the Mk.VB. This introduced two 20mm guns and four .303 guns and a long range belly tank for extending their range. With this aircraft the Northolt Wing of Spitfires, as they had now been called, became very well known and feared by the enemy. One of the biggest fighter sweeps of 1941 took place on 7th August. Circus 62 was an attack on a power station at Lille by six Blenheim bombers. They were to be escorted by 18 Spitfire and two Hurricane squadrons. Two squadrons of the Northolt Wing were waiting above the French coast to protect the bombers' withdrawal. As they waited for the Blenheims to appear, Nos 306 and 308 were suddenly pounced on by 18 Me 109s with sadly, two Spitfires being shot down.

With the increasing tempo in offensive operations, there were bound to be losses. The new Air Officer Commanding No 11 Group, Air Vice-Marshal Trafford Leigh-Mallory, could not accept the number of casualties resulting from Circus operations. By the autumn he had the backing of Winston Churchill and by November 1941, the sweeps had ceased.

Prior to this time, No 303 (Kosciusko) Polish Squadron had been moved to Speke near Liverpool for a rest. They had been on offensive operations from Northolt since the new year, but the rest was to be shortlived as they came back to the base on 7th October flying the Spitfire VB and commanded by one of their own kinsmen, Squadron Leader J. Jankiewicz, VM, KW, DFC.

On 7th December 1941, Japan attacked Pearl Harbor and on the 11th, the United States declared war on Italy and Germany. The repercussions of such a momentous event had little impact on Northolt with the exception that at last, perhaps, the war would begin to go our way. Christmas that year was celebrated with certainly a better feeling than the last. With the plans for a landing at Dieppe being formulated, 1942 was to be a year of change.

The opening of the year saw 315, 316 and 317 Polish Squadrons still in residence, No 308 having departed to Woodvale just prior to Christmas. The next few months were a continuous round of escort and offensive operations but as July approached, a plan was being drawn up that in Churchill's words would 'test the enemy defences on a strongly defended sector of coast'. The town of Dieppe lay in a mile wide gap at the mouth of the River D'Arques. It was known that the area was heavily defended, but

Two British Waafs join a pilot of No 308 Polish Squadron on the engine cowling of his Spitfire, Northolt 1942. (RAF Northolt)

it was hoped that tactical surprise and the best planning possible would overcome this resistance. Codenamed Operation Rutter, the name was changed to 'Jubilee' after an unsuccessful exercise, perhaps a forewarning of what was to come.

The date planned for the landings was 18th August 1942. In the event, bad weather postponed the sailing of the invasion force for 24 hours. On the night of 18th August, 252 ships of all descriptions sailed to arrive unseen off the coast of Dieppe in the early hours of the 19th. The object of the RAF during these landings was to provide close support and also to lure the Luftwaffe into the air with the intention of destroying it. Two hours prior to the landings, the Polish squadrons had begun a softening up process by attacking the enemy beyond the Dieppe beaches and town. Flying many sorties over the two days, Northolt was entering a very busy period.

Prior to 'Jubilee', in April 315 had left for Woodvale and July

A Spitfire of 317 Squadron covered in messages to their friends – written in chalk easily removed. (RAF Northolt)

saw 316 leave for Hutton Cranswick, with 317 returning to Northolt from Croydon. No 306 came back from Kirton-in-Lindsey on 16th June in time for the operation which saw both resident Polish squadrons in action for many hours. As they flew over the troops below who were attempting to get ashore under very heavy gunfire from the enemy, it appeared at first that the Luftwaffe was very reluctant to appear.

By 10 am on the 19th all this had changed when large formations of the new Focke-Wulf 190 arrived over Dieppe. Below, the 2nd Canadian Division were struggling to get a foothold beyond the beach. One hour after the assault craft had landed them, the Royal Marine Commandos and men from various units of the British Army came under intense enemy fire which held them back and in the end forced a retreat back to the waiting ships. Above, the Polish Spitfires tangled with the superior Fw 190s. With their time over the beach-head limited by fuel, they returned to Northolt to refuel and rearm before flying back to the fray, witnessing the carnage that was happening on the beach below.

A potent enemy – the Focke-Wulfe Fw 190A. (MAP)

The troops were pinned down on the beach by the most ferocious of enemy fire whilst the guns of the German medium and heavy batteries engaged the British ships offshore. Heavy casualties resulted and a few hours after the landings had been made, the decision was made to withdraw – but not before the Canadians had lost a third of their entire force and the rest of the armies around 4,300 men. Dieppe had turned out to be a massacre.

For Northolt, the next few days came as a welcome respite. The two Polish squadrons claimed 16 aircraft destroyed for no losses which considering that they were up against the Fw 190, a fighter later described as the best fighter Germany ever produced, was very satisfactory. Sadly however, Operation Jubilee had cost the RAF 106 aircraft, against the Luftwaffe losing 48.

The weeks after Dieppe came as an anti-climax with the RAF coming up against the Fw 190 more and more. This was still the period of the fighter/bomber attacks, low level to the English coast to avoid radar detection then low level across Kent or Sussex to drop their bombs and head for home. Once again there was a change in the Polish squadrons as 315 returned on 5th September 1942 from Woodvale and converted to the Spitfire IX

166

whilst 317 replaced them at Woodvale. 315, now led by Squadron Leader M. Wiorkiewicz, soon became fully involved in carrying out Rodeos and Ramrods. As autumn approached, the high intensity operations became less frequent but there was still plenty of 'Hun hunting' to be had across the Channel.

By this time, several of the smaller units that had been at Northolt began coming to the fore. A Special Service Flight was formed at Northolt in October 1942 in an attempt to combat the high flying Ju 86Rs that could reach a ceiling of some 45,000 feet. This took it beyond the reach of nearly all Allied fighters at this time but the Spitfire IX, in a modified version, could reach this height to deal with the new menace. Stripped of all its armour and carrying just two 20mm cannons, the first successful interception of a Ju 86 was when Pilot Officer Prince Emmanual Galitzine, a Russian born pilot, damaged one over Southampton before low fuel forced him to return to Northolt.

The other unit to deserve recognition was the Defiant Flight, which had been operating from Northolt and Heston since the end of the Battle of Britain. On 1st October 1942, they were formed into a permanent flight at Northolt and were tasked with the then very secret process of developing a jamming system for the enemy radar beams. They worked in conjunction with the A&AEE at Boscombe Down and the TRE at Defford. The status of squadron strength was granted soon after and the flight became No 515 Squadron. On many occasions during their stay at Northolt or Heston, they would be airborne, ahead of the large bomber force now carrying the war back to Germany. With their electronic equipment, they would jam the enemy radars giving the bombers a better chance to deliver their bombload unheeded and return safely. The unit moved to Hunsdon in June 1943 after carrying out sterling work at Northolt.

As 1943 dawned, Northolt was still home to the Polish squadrons. On a global scale, the 8th Army was pushing Rommel out of the war and there was talk of a second front within the next year. No 315 (Deblin) Squadron were now flying the mark Vb Spitfire but their time at Northolt was limited and they left, not to return, on 2nd June 1943. This left 317 to continue the long Polish association with the station, but they too were to leave for Southend at the end of the year.

167

A pilot of 303 Polish Squadron is scrambled at Northolt during 1943.
(RAF Northolt)

No 124 (Baroda) Squadron had adopted the motto 'Danger is our opportunity', which they certainly lived up to. With their high flying and pressurised Spitfire VIs, they absorbed the Special Service flight into their ranks and carried on the high interception sorties against the Ju 86s, averaging at least one destruction a month.

The autumn of 1943 brought big changes to the structure of Fighter Command, with the intensive offensive operations continuing at a vast pace and the prospect of an Allied landing in France during 1944. On 13th November 1943, the Allied Expeditionary Air Force came into existence with Air Chief-Marshal Leigh-Mallory as its commanding officer. This new air force would comprise the American 9th Air Force, the 2nd Tactical Air Force and the Air Defence of Great Britain. The 2nd TAF took 32 fighter squadrons from the old Fighter Command including those at Northolt. However, by this time, 124 had moved down to West Malling and the remaining Polish squadrons had been sent north to rest. The base seemed

Some of the Polish squadrons were later equipped with the North American Mustang. Here, a Mk. I powered by the lower rated Allison engines belongs to No 2 Squadron. Later marks had a Rolls-Royce Merlin power plant. (IWM)

strangely quiet without the constant roar of Merlin engines, but the Poles returned later that year, leaving again in December for Rochford. Staying for just two weeks, they were back at Northolt this time remaining until April 1944. However, with just one squadron in residence, the days of Northolt as a fighter station were numbered.

Being the closest airfield to Stanmore and Uxbridge, Northolt became the command's main terminal and as such was earmarked for expansion. The first requirement was for a longer runway and work began on extending the main north-east/south-west runway and later the smaller north/south runway. These extensions would herald a new use for the station but it was to remain a fighter base until April 1944. During that month, the long association with the Polish squadrons ended as the last one, 317, moved down to the Advanced Landing Ground at Deanland in preparation for D-Day. (See *Sussex Airfields in the Second World War*.) Although it had not received the attention of

169

the Luftwaffe like the other 11 Group airfields had, nor had it received the glory, Northolt had played a vital part in the greatest aerial battle ever undertaken. Now it was to enter a new phase, that of accommodating transport aircraft.

The association with fighters was not entirely severed for the station became a forward airfield in the Tangmere sector. It did lose its sector status but already the formation of the air force was changing as it prepared for peace, and there was no longer a case for Northolt to be a sector station. It was however used extensively by No 16 Photographic Reconnaissance Squadron who brought their Spitfire XIs in on 16th April 1944, and also by No 140 Photographic Reconnaissance Squadron who flew the first Mosquitos to use Northolt in from Hartford Bridge at the same time.

One month later, No 69 Squadron reassembled at the base as part of No 34 Wing of the 2nd TAF. It flew the Vickers Wellington XIII, one of the many variants of this amazing bomber. As D-Day, 6th June 1944 approached, the Wellingtons were tasked with flying over the beaches of Normandy dropping flares to help locate enemy troop movements. This operation continued up to and beyond the successful landings in France and they remained at Northolt until September 1944 when they moved over to France and Belgium as the German army was pushed back to the Rhine. At least the station was able to play a part in the largest invasion in history.

The closing months of the war saw the strategic role of Northolt grow. It now became the ADGB Communications station and was used by many VIPs as well as being one of the main reception centres for the German prisoners captured as the Allies continued to push further into France. The transport aircraft movements grew to enormous proportions as Northolt was now rapidly becoming known as London's main airport. One of the last units to be based there as August 1945 approached was a detachment of No 271 Squadron whose five Dakotas were to stay until the end of the war to operate scheduled passenger services to Brussels.

With the end of hostilities, the transport use continued and together with an increase in civilian flights using the facilities, Northolt was to play an important role in transport and

In memory of the brave fallen Polish airmen, RAF Northolt.

171

communications. Today, in this world of a rapidly shrinking air force, it is still an important military base and is home to the Northolt Station flight operating an Islander aircraft and No 32 (The Royal Squadron) operating such aircraft as the Bae 125, Bae 146 and the Squirrel and Wessex helicopters. From the First World War to the Second and into peacetime, Northolt has always been and will remain, a very important military airfield.

10

OAKLEY

By April 1945 with victory just around the corner, many of the larger training airfields in the region were made ready to receive thousands of liberated prisoners of war. What began as the few soon became the many and the volume of air traffic generated by Operation Exodus increased tenfold. As in the Berlin Airlift that was to come later, sometimes upward of 100 aircraft would be in various stages of flight at one time. With large aircraft such as Lancasters and Stirlings and small aircraft such as Mosquitos and Ansons all plying for a position in the air and on the ground, the larger airfields in the area saw far more movements during June and July 1945 than they had ever done. One of the airfields used in Operation Exodus was Oakley.

A satellite of Westcott, the airfield was ready for operations before the parent airfield. Officially opened on 27th May 1942, it was deemed a second satellite of Bicester. However, with the completion of Westcott, Oakley became its main satellite airfield.

The layout was the usual pattern for a Bomber Command OTU with a three runway configuration. Several T2 hangars were erected, together with a rather unusual B1 hangar. A Ministry of Aircraft Production design, it encompassed a larger ground area and a greater angle on the roof than the other hangars to allow it to accommodate bomber aircraft for major servicing. Domestic and ancillary buildings abounded around the perimeter together with the usual dispersal areas.

With No 11 OTU arriving at Westcott on 28th September 1942, the Wellington Ics used for the gunnery training of flights B and D moved into Oakley. The pattern of training ran very similar to Westcott with aircrew of all categories living together and sorting themselves into crews, which would consist of a pilot, navigator, bomb aimer, wireless operator and rear gunner. With this done, the training commenced on the Wellington. Most of the pilots would previously have flown smaller twin-engined aircraft such as the Airspeed Oxford or the Avro Anson. To convert to the Wellington, it was necessary to first fly with a qualified instructor doing 'circuits and bumps' before attempting a series of solo flights. These would be by day at first, later progressing to night flying, but all of this brought the usual spate of accidents, some minor but many major with tragic results.

Some of the problems were connected with the lack of power in the Bristol Pegasus engines fitted in the Wellington Ic, and such a case in question happened at Oakley when a Wellington flown by Flight Lieutenant S. Manning suffered an engine failure on take-off. Had the aircraft been the Wellington III or the Mark X with the Bristol Hercules engines, the aircraft may well have been able to continue in flight on one engine but a failure on the Ic usually resulted in a crash. With one engine out, the pilot gave full power to the remaining one in the hope of continuing his climb. It was to no avail and being just over the threshold of the runway, it seemed a crash landing was inevitable. However, skilfully manoeuvering his aircraft, Manning managed to turn the Wellington through a 180 degree turn and land downwind on the runway from which he had just left. The incident, however, was not entirely without mishap as the Wellington actually struck some trees at the end of the runway which caused considerable damage to the nose and bomb bay, but no injuries to any of the crew.

At the other end of the spectrum was a bad accident which occurred on 1st May 1943, which is indicative of many similar.

The local bombing range used by the aircraft of 11 OTU was situated at Charlton-on-Otmoor and on this particular day Wellington 8866 (XM-X), flown by Sergeant Richmond, had been

The Wellington flown by Flight Sergeant S.H. Manning which collided with trees after an abortive take-off at Oakley. (S Manning via J. Hampton)

over the range dropping practice bombs. Carrying out the operation successfully, the crew left the range and prepared to return to Oakley. Several minutes later, the aircraft crashed at Belchers Farm, Stadhampton. All five members of the crew perished and although the bombing range at the time reported to Oakley seeing a fire in the distance, the reason for the tragedy was never clearly defined.

It was ironic that two weeks earlier, the same crew had suffered a similar problem but with different results. On this occasion, the aircraft was returning from a night sortie when shortly after midnight, the Wellington suffered a port engine failure. After instructing the rear gunner, Sergeant Cheetham, to bale out, Sergeant Richmond, the pilot, managed to crashland his aircraft in a field near Rickmansworth without loss of life. Cheetham, not knowing what had happened to the aircraft and its crew, upon landing ran to the nearest telephone and contacted

Staff at 'A' Flight, Oakley: standing, l to r – Fl/Lt A.H. Fernihough DFC, RAF; W/O T. Paul, RNZAF; F/O D. Willett DFM, RAAF; F/O D.F. Walker, RNZAF; F/Sgt J. Wild, RAF; P/O A. Hopley, RAF; F/O W.M. Sellars, RNZAF. Sitting, l to r – Fl/Lt G.A. Morley, RAF; Fl/Lt G. Gunn, RNZAF; P/O D.Edwards, RAF. (S Manning via J. Hampton)

Oakley. Three-quarters of an hour later, Richmond also contacted Oakley to report that he had crashlanded and needed transport to pick him and the crew up. They could never have known that after this happy ending, two weeks later they would all die in a similar incident.

Being a full-size bomber airfield, aircraft returning from bombing raids over enemy territory and in trouble, would often divert to Oakley. These diversions became known as 'Cuckoos' for obvious reasons and included American as well as British aircraft. Both the parent station and Oakley were capable of handling the very largest aircraft of the period. As an example, the night of 5th April 1944 was a very busy one when eight Lancasters of No 106 Squadron landed after a raid on Toulouse. With hardly any room for other operations that night, the Lancasters departed to their home base next morning. Again, on 7th June 1944 at 02.30 in the morning, a Halifax in trouble radioed Oakley for permission to carry out an emergency landing. Before

More staff of 'A' Flight; l to r – W/O N. Gustofson, RNZAF; Fl/Lt N. Hall, RAF; F/Sgt A. Hollingsworth, RAF. Sitting l to r – F/O D. Willett DFM, RAAF; P/O S. Manning, RNZAF. (S. Manning via J. Hampton)

it could begin its approach, the captain ordered his crew to bale out and the aircraft crashed near Benson airfield. Even this late in the war, tragedy was never far away.

Although Oakley's primary role was as a satellite to Westcott, it carried out much of the conversion training for 11 OTU. As we have read, with the end of the war it became home to thousands of repatriated prisoners. After the traumas and terrors of the German prison camps, many of them returned emaciated. Oakley offered them their first real meal and taste of sanity in years in what was to become for many, a long period of adjustment to normal life.

With the repatriation over, the airfield closed to flying in August 1945 and no more use was made of the satellite. Many of those who underwent training at Oakley later perished on operational flights over enemy territory. To quote the official Air Ministry figures, the casualties suffered by Bomber Command were: Dead 55,573; Wounded 8,403; POW 9,838; Missing but later safe 2,951; Total 76,765. It was a great sacrifice, but the figures could have been much worse were it not for Operational Training Units such as Oakley.

Today most of the airfield has returned to agricultural use, but parts of the area can most certainly be distinguished as a wartime base.

11

THAME

Though perhaps a rather mundane airfield compared to many others, Thame in Buckinghamshire was none the less an important training airfield. Previously known as Haddenham, it became an RAF Glider Pilot Training airfield in the latter days of 1940 when it was enlarged over a period of some months.

Officially opened in January 1941, bad weather had hampered the workmen but by the 11th of the month, the completed Bessoneaux hangars and three domestic huts were ready for use. The landing area had been obstructed some months before lest enemy paratroopers arrived. The removal of some of the items took time and had only just been completed when on 13th January, Squadron Leader Lomax, the Senior Medical Officer of No 70 Group, arrived to inspect the site to confirm that it was fit for habitation. Although still far from complete, with the acquisition of several barns and outbuildings belonging to the local landowners, it was deemed habitable.

On 16th January 1941, several Kirby Kite Sailplanes arrived by road and were immediately placed in the hangars. The arrival of Squadron Leader H.E. Hervey, MC as Officer Commanding Glider Training, indicated that the airfield was soon to be active, this being substantiated by the arrival of several Tiger Moths. Thame now became a unit encompassed within No 23 Group, Flying Training Command.

With the early spring bringing the better weather, the training of pilots began. Soon the sight of a Tiger Moth towing a Kirby Kite became a familiar pattern around the local area. One of the tasks allotted to Thame was to obtain information on fighter tactics should the enemy attack glider formations. Exercises were carried out jointly with the Air Fighting Development Unit stationed at Duxford, one of which took place on 5th February 1941.

As dawn broke, five Tiger Moths with gliders were prepared for the second of such exercises. With the groundcrews carrying out the basic checks needed for towing, the weather report was collected from Halton by 8 am with the briefing scheduled for 10 am. With a good weather report, the crews were ready for take-off at 10.45 am and rolling across the grass, they were safely airborne and heading for a rendezvouz with the AFDU at a position west of Royston near Duxford. The aircraft and crews concerned with the exercise were as follows:

Tiger Moth N9347 (F/O Gardiner and Sqd/Ldr Hervey) towing Kite A (P/O Fender).
Tiger Moth T5063 (Fl/Lt Saffery and F/O Sproule) towing Kite B (F/O Davis).
Tiger Moth N9198 (P/O Montefiore) towing Kite K (Sgt Furlong).
Tiger Moth N9197 (P/O Grieg and P/O Wright) towing Kite D (F/O Wilkinson).
Tiger Moth T5417 (Sgt Smith and CQMS Dixon) towing Kite E (Cpl Ruffle).

The exercise proved that indeed, gliders could sometimes outfly the enemy and at the conclusion, both tugs and gliders returned safely to Thame having successfully evaded the enemy!

It was, however, further felt that to really get an idea of how gliders would respond to an enemy attack, properly constructed gliders and not sailplanes, should be used. It was equally felt by all the instructors and pupils at Thame that flying sailplanes was not really equipping them for the real job of flying gliders. Accordingly, after much discussion, 14th October 1941 saw the first of six General Aircraft Hotspurs arrive at Thame. This

Signing a Form 700 for a training flight in a Hotspur glider. The aircraft was mainly used in the training role at Thame and Theale. (IWM)

aircraft eventually became the standard training glider throughout the war and though intended to be used operationally, in service it was found to be inadequate for the intended purpose. The instructors and pupils at Thame, however, welcomed the prospect of flying them. With the new gliders came a selection of basically obsolete aircraft to tow them. Hawker Hectors and Hinds and even two Avro 504Ns were given a resurgence of life for the purpose and in the role, served the GTS well.

Although for the most part of its war, Thame carried on its training in comparative peace, several incidents brought the realities of war closer to the instructors and pupils. One such incident happened on 7th September 1942 when a Douglas Havoc which had been taking part in a Turbinlite operation, crashed at 9.45 pm in a field a short distance from the airfield. Suffering from engine trouble, Pilot Officer Burnet-Smith had told his two-man crew to bale out. This they did successfully, descending safely to land in a field nearby. Struggling with the controls, Burnet-Smith carried out a controlled crash-landing, but sadly suffered first and second degree burns to his face and hands when the aircraft caught fire. Thame had had its first taste of war.

By late 1942, in addition to training glider pilots, a school for glider instructors was established. Several new aircraft arrived to act in the tug role, one of them being the Miles Master. Developed from the earlier Miles Kestrel trainer, it had been designed as a high speed trainer. Its reception once in service, however, was luke-warm and it was later adopted for glider towing. Despite its failure as a trainer, 3,301 aircraft were built, the last being in late 1942. It served in the glider towing role well and was certainly a more powerful aircraft for the job than the Tiger Moth.

Several more incidents occurred at Thame. The first was when a Tiger Moth flew into high tension cables at Meadle near Aylesbury. The weather was appalling at the time and in order to get below a rapidly descending cloud base, the pilot had lost altitude quickly. Hitting the cables, the aircraft fell to the ground, sadly killing the two pilots, one army and one RAF. Later that same day, Sergeant White crash-landed a Hawker Hind at 5 pm in the middle of the landing area. Luckily he sustained no injuries.

Again, on 21st October 1942, an early morning training sortie ended in disaster with a Miles Master towing a Kirby Kite. Somehow the tow rope became disengaged and the glider crashed on take-off. The two pilots undergoing training, Pilot Officer J.A. Hawkins and Flight Sergeant A.P. Collins sustained multiple injuries. On the 25th of the same month, another incident involving a Master and a glider resulted in the death of Flight Lieutenant C.F.C. Ridout and injuries to Pilot Officer R. Beamish. Even in the relative seclusion of a training station, death and injury were never far away.

By November and despite the first snow warning being received, since the commencement of training aircraft from Thame had carried out 780 flights consisting of 428 tug hours and 225 gliding hours. The year ended on a bad note when the Hawker Hector of Sergeant Edmonds crashed on the south side of the airfield after releasing its glider. The aircraft came to rest on its back with the pilot trapped beneath. Only very prompt action by the two glider pilots, Sergeants Gabbot and Westerby, who had landed instantly and who pulled the unconscious pilot out, had saved him from possible death.

The new year of 1943 saw the Glider Instructors School move to Shobden as the airfield was handed over to the Ministry of Aircraft Production. The reason given was that Thame was too small for the larger gliders that were now coming into production, and a search for a larger airfield resulted in the training school moving to Croughton in Northamptonshire. Thame had served its purpose well but with the departure of the gliding school, was to remain non-operational for the rest of 1942.

A resurgence of use came in early 1943 when the Royal Naval Air Experimental Department was formed for target towing. A wide variety of naval aircraft now flew from the airfield including Martinets, Swordfish and Vengeance. The unit remained until May 1945 when they were replaced by the 3rd Reception Centre of the RAF. They left five months later, leaving Thame in the hands of the RAF Radio Engineers until 30th April 1946 when the airfield closed as a military base. It was further used by civilian aircraft engineers with part of the airfield becoming an industrial site. Thame is now an unlicensed aerodrome, but sailplaining still takes place on a limited scale.

12

WELFORD

When the wartime programme for airfield requirements was drawn up in August 1940, it was proposed to site the majority of bomber OTUs in the Midlands. Over the course of further planning, some came into the Thames Valley region. It was further suggested that bomber OTUs should have a second satellite and that a total of 43 OTUs would be necessary in the UK. This was enough to equip the RAF whilst any surplus airfields went to the USAAF. One of these surplus airfields was Welford.

Situated seven miles north-west of Newbury in Berkshire, the airfield was built on a flat area of land close to the River Lambourne. Authorised in October 1941 as an OTU, building commenced immediately after the land had been requisitioned from local landowners. It was built to a standard bomber airfield pattern with a three runway layout, the main one of 2,000 feet being aligned north-west/south-east. Two T-Type hangars were built together with a total of 50 aircraft hardstandings consisting of 46 loops and four pans. Accommodation and technical sites were situated within the airfield boundary as the thinking was that Welford, so far from the area of enemy action, would not be of interest to the Luftwaffe. It had already been earmarked for No 92 Group, Bomber Command and was also classified as a second satellite to Membury.

Taking until 21st April 1943 to be completed, it was No 70

Group RAF that accepted responsibility for RAF Welford. By 10th June the forward party had arrived to set up the SHQ but already Welford had been allocated to the USAAF. This became official in July and by 6th September 1943, the Americans had arrived and Welford became US Station 474 (Welford Park).

Once again, as with all the bomber OTUs handed over to the USAAF within the area, the base was to become a Troop Carrier Wing. Nothing happened until November when the remnants of the 315th TCG arrived from nearby Aldermaston. Welford Park came to near full capacity one month later when the 434th TCG (71st, 72nd, 73rd and 74th TCS) arrived from Fulbeck. Flying C-47s, they commenced an intensive training period with gliders and troops.

They returned to Fulbeck after a short stay and were replaced by the 435th TCG (75th, 76th, 77th and 78th TCS). Commanded by Colonel Frank J. MacNees, the 435th also commenced a period of training. They were joined by the 438th TCG (87th, 88th, 89th and 90th TCS) later in the month, also flying C-47s. Welford Park suddenly seemed very crowded with personnel and aircraft. With little rest from training over the festive period, both units transferred to the 9th Air Force on 22nd February 1944. The 438th moved over to Greenham Common on 16th March leaving Welford Park to the 435th TCG and the US 101st Airborne Division.

Crest of the 435th Troop Carrier Group, Welford Park. (C Samson)

185

With the planning for 'Overlord' at an advanced stage, the C-47s and C-53 transport aircraft began practice tows with US Waco CG-4A and British Airspeed Horsa gliders. It was with the success of the German airborne forces sweeping through Norway, Belgium and Holland during the summer of 1940, that the training of airborne forces in Britain had been given a priority. The use of gliders for carrying troops started when the Central Landing School was formed at Ringway, Manchester. Later the gliding training section was split off to become No 1 Glider Training School at RAF Croughton in Northants.

Between 1940 and 1945, over 1,000 training gliders and over 4,000 operational gliders were produced in Britain for the RAF. Others were supplied by the Americans, with the first British airborne operations with gliders (over Norway) taking place on 19th November 1942 and the last (across the Rhine) in March 1945. Of the two types of gliders used in the training and eventual assault on France, the Horsa had a crew of two and could carry 20 to 25 troops. The other type used in the assault

A Horsa glider of the 101st Airborne Division lands at dawn on a field at Welford, 12th May 1944. (Signal Corps)

was the American Waco Hadrian glider, which was considerably smaller. First supplied to the RAF in 1943, they were used in the Allied invasion of Sicily in July 1943. This was their only use in RAF operations, but the Americans continued to use them for 'Overlord' and for the intensive training programme at Welford Park and other bases.

As the rehearsal for the assault gathered pace, Welford Park played host to Mr Churchill and General Eisenhower. They arrived when 97 gliders were being towed off on a formation, cross-country exercise. After release at a designated place, they all returned to the airfield precisely on time, a perfect demonstration of just how efficient the carriers and the airborne forces had become.

As 6th June approached, an intense security cordon was thrown around Welford Park. Shortly after midnight on 5th June, the familiar drone of hundreds of aircraft engines above the south coast of England caused people to lift the black-out curtains of their rooms and peer up at the sky. For months, the noise of engines around the Thames Valley area had been heard departing and returning. However, on this particular night, the sound was more intense and did not return until much later than usual. Operation Overlord had begun.

As dawn approached on the 6th, the 435th with its troops left Welford Park to carry out the first wave of paratroop drops. Men of the 101st Airborne Divisional Headquarters, including the Divisional Commander, Major-General Maxwell D. Taylor, together with the 2nd Battalion 501st Parachute Infantry Regiment were dropped at designated zones near Cherbourg. Cloud cover over the beaches caused a few problems but the drop in the main was successful. Three C-47s and their gliders were lost to enemy action with seven more damaged. These were able to land back at base and after being repaired, were sent once again to tow more gliders and troops. The towing operations continued throughout the next day but with airstrips on the Continent now rapidly becoming available to the Allies, the despatching of medical supplies, food and ammunition became the priority. Landing at the hastily made strips, the C-47s brought back the wounded to Welford Park who were then taken to hospitals in the Newbury area.

Part of the vast Allied airborne army which participated in the invasion of

Holland, preparing to board their transport planes, 1944. (National Archives)

The sky was filled with paratroops as D-Day drew near. (SE Newspapers)

A BBC war correspondent gives us the flavour of the operation in his own words: 'From where I am, standing between the two pilots of this glider, I can see the navigation lights of the tug in front of us and off to the left and right, the navigation lights of other tugs and other gliders bound on the same mission. Circling above from time to time, I can see the lights of the fighter screen which is protecting us. And looking back down the glider, there are seated, although I can hardly see them in the half light, officers and men all laden with equipment so heavy that they can barely walk. They have to carry with them items with which they can fight the moment they land. We are over the enemy coast now and the run-in has started. One minute. Thirty seconds. Red light. Green light. Out, out. Get out! Out into the cool night. Out into the area over France but we know the dropping zone is obstructed. We are in fact jumping into fields that are covered in poles. But I hit my chute and lower my kit bag which is suspended on the end of a 40 foot rope from my harness. And then the ground comes up to hit me and I find myself in the middle of a cornfield. Suddenly all hell is let loose as the enemy realise what is happening. There is firing all around us and we throw ourselves to the ground. This is D-Day in France.'

The words of General Eisenhower, the Supreme Commander of the Allied Forces, did however bring a ray of hope to the oppressed: 'People of Western Europe. A landing was made this morning on the coast of France by troops of the Allied Expeditionary Force. This landing is a part of a United Nations plan for the liberation of Europe, made in conjunction with our great Russian allies. I have this message for all of you. Although the initial assault may not have been made in your own country, the hour of your liberation is approaching.'

The foothold in Europe had been gained and Welford Park had played an important part in its success. For its part in 'Overlord', the 435th received a Distinguished Unit Citation. There was, however, no rest for the 435th TCG as a detachment was sent to Italy to participate in Operation Anvil, the amphibious assault on

Preparation for an aerial resupply exercise for American troops of the 101st AD. (Signal Corps)

southern France. The aircraft remained until the end of August when they flew back to Welford Park and into another period of intensive training.

The remainder of the unit began transport services following the landings and intermittently were engaged in missions of that type until VE Day. In addition they delivered supplies such as serum, blood plasma, radar sets, clothing, rations and ammunition before evacuating wounded personnel to Allied hospitals. For the 435th and the 101st Airborne, the next operation was 'Market Garden', the ill-fated invasion to capture vital river bridges in Holland.

As we have seen from other chapters, it was a gamble that did not quite pay off. 'Market Garden' began in the early hours of 17th September 1944 and just after 10 am on the same day, 36 C-47s were rolling down the runway of Welford Park towing gliders containing paratroops of the 101st Airborne to drop just north of the Wilhelmina Canal near Eindhoven. The routes were marked by beacons and coded lights on Channel shipping. Full air cover was provided by around 1,000 British and American fighters although the greatest danger came from flak. The sheer ferocity of this brought down two C-47s and damaged ten more in the first sortie whilst another eight were damaged in the second.

Over the drop zone, the C-47s released their gliders which landed very accurately. Gathering together their fire-power, the 101st very soon captured the two southern bridges between Veghel and Eindhoven. This initial success, however, was not to be applied to the other forces who met heavy resistance directly they landed. Whilst history records that 'Market Garden' was not a total failure due to the securing of two passages across the Maas and Waal Canals, many good lives were lost and their sacrifice marked the end of any hopes of ending the war in 1944.

As the C-47s returned to Welford Park, some badly damaged, thoughts turned to those who would not be coming back. The next two days saw further glider tows together with supply drops. 'Market Garden' finally closed on 25th September with the evacuation of the surviving paratroops. There was, however, no slowing of the pace as during mid December, the enemy launched a major offensive through the Ardennes in eastern

Belgium. With the 101st Airborne encircled around the town of Bastogne, the C-47s from Welford Park and other bases kept up the job of resupplying them until they were able to be relieved.

As 1945 dawned, the 435th prepared to move to Bretigny in France. After a very successful time at Welford Park and with victory in sight at last, the fight was being carried back to the Continent. The 435th moved back to the United States in August 1945 and were in-activated on 15th November before being placed on the reserve list. After many years as a base of the USAAF, Welford Park was returned to the RAF in June 1945 and reverted to the name of Welford.

Taken over by Transport Command, No 1336 (Transport Support) Conversion Unit was formed at Welford on 30th June 1945. Courses began in August with Dakotas and Horsas, these continuing until 1st March 1946 when the unit was cut. Welford was then reduced to Care and Maintenance for a short period before transferring to No 90 (Signals) Group in October 1946. The association with flying did not entirely stop at this point thanks to the enterprise of a local company. Elliots of Newbury had designed and built the Eon, a four-seat light aeroplane, during 1946/7. Looking for a site from which to test fly it, they approached the Air Ministry with a view to using Welford. With permission granted, they commenced flight trials in August 1947. The company was joined by the headquarters of the Southern Signals Areas which had formed at Welford at the same time. Both Elliots and the headquarters stayed for around two years despite the transfer of the airfield from a signals group to Maintenance Command in 1950. Reduced to Care and Maintenance once again on 1st August 1952, it was to remain this way for two years.

New life was breathed into the airfield in 1955 when it was accepted, once again, as a logistics base for the USAAF. With an intense security cordon being installed around Welford and the construction of underground bunkers, a munitions depot took over the entire site. It became the main ammunition dump for all the American bases in the UK and remains this way today, controlled by the 100th Regional Support Group for the 20th Fighter Wing of the 3rd Air Force. It gave valuable support to NATO throughout the 'cold war' period and in 1991, the base and personnel of the 850th Munitions Maintenance Squadron USAF, along with British service and civilian staff, made a significant contribution to the Allied victory in the Gulf War. On 1st April 1995, RAF Welford became a joint use facility co-operated by the USAF 424th Air Base Squadron and the Royal Air Force.

In remembrance of all the units that served at Welford, a memorial was erected in 1993 close to the entrance. In this world of ever diminishing air forces, including the USA, is it possible that Welford will remain a military base?

13

WESTCOTT

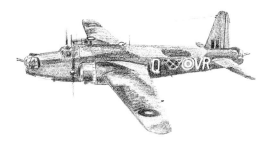

Out of the four main wartime RAF commands, it was Bomber Command that was first to establish Operational Training Units. During the initial months of the war, Arthur 'Bomber' Harris, then the AOC of No 5 Group, came up with the idea of utilising parts of aircraft which were surplus to requirements.

His idea involved using sections of aircraft to recreate an operational environment. Each section was individual, ie a nose, a middle and a tail section into which was placed a crew member according to his trade. The pilot would then be installed in the Link Trainer and connected by intercom to the various other members of the crew. It became known as 'The Dummy Fuselage Scheme' and was the forerunner of today's simulators. 'Bomber' Harris himself wrote: 'The individuals and finally the whole crews will be put through this procedure time and time again until they are procedure perfect.' Many OTUs were to benefit from the scheme and it certainly gave the crews a good insight into operational life.

In September 1942, a Wellington fuselage was installed in a hangar at Westcott airfield and the OTU began its first simulator training. A similar simulator designed to train both pilots and bomb aimers was later installed at the satellite airfield at Oakley. Known as the Air Ministry Bombing Teacher, a pilot would sit at the controls whilst the bomb aimer would sit below giving instructions for the bombing of a target which was projected on to a screen below.

On 21st April 1941, the requirements for OTUs were changed. Each OTU airfield would now have a satellite and the intake would be 45 pilots at each OTU every two weeks along with 40 wireless operators/air gunners and 20 each of air gunners/observers. Like the rest of the OTUs in the area, Westcott was to receive Wellington Ics. These arrived in the shape of No 11 OTU during September and October 1942.

The airfield was situated ten miles east-southeast of Bicester in Buckinghamshire, and in addition to 11 OTU was also home to the Electronic Countermeasures Development Unit of 92 Group which also used Wellingtons for its radio electronic trials. Previously agricultural land, it was very damp in places. Once the site was cleared, five hangars were constructed together with all the usual buildings associated with a bomber station.

Wing Commander E.J. Little, DFC, RAF arrived to assume command, but quickly handed over the reins to Group Captain R.W.P. Collings, AFC, RAF on 2nd October 1942. Westcott had the satellite at Oakley which from the beginning accommodated B and D Gunnery Flights whilst the parent station had A and C Gunnery Flights. The instructors were men who had completed at least one operational tour whilst the trainees were already aircrew but came to Westcott for bombing training before joining an operational squadron. Aircrew training began immediately with the Station Diarist recording that ammunition expenditure at the 1st October 1942 stood at: Air to Air – 183,400 rounds; Air to Ground – 17,000 rounds.

Though some distance from London, the occasional enemy aircraft did stray as far as Westcott. One such occasion took place in the early evening of 17th January 1943 when the Oxford Observer Corps reported to Westcott control that enemy raiders had been seen 20 miles away travelling westward. The station went to Air Raid Warning Red, attack imminent, and the flarepath was hastily extinguished. However, although aircraft engines were heard in the distance, no raiders entered the Westcott zone and the 'all clear' sounded two hours later. Shortly after this, Group Captain Collings left to be replaced by Group Captain R.S. Shaw, DFC, RAuxAF.

As with all OTUs, accidents were inevitable. On 15th March 1943 at 10.55, Wellington Q, s/n 9792 of C flight and flown by Sergeant Lawson, was returning from a cross-country exercise codenamed 'Bullseye'. Approaching Westcott, the pilot realised that he was too high to land and prepared to overshoot. Climbing steeply, the aircraft stalled and crashed on the north-eastern end of the north-east/south-west runway. The impact caused the Wellington to catch fire, sadly consuming the entire crew before the crash crews could reach the site. Another accident in which the entire crew perished happened on 2nd May 1943 when a Wellington returning from bombing practice at the Charlton-on-Otmoor range, crashed at Belchers Farm, Stadhampton. It was never found just what caused the accident, but all five members of the crew were killed. These are just two examples of many similar incidents.

The duty of the Station Diarist was to daily record all such incidents, both serious and humorous. On 31st May, it was recorded that owing to the high price now allowed for swill, pigs were to be kept on the station and fed on the swill from the airmen's and officers' messes. Any profit would be credited to the PSI funds, yet in the same week the 'Wings for Victory' campaign reported a substantial increase in War Savings, the total reaching £6,180. Was it coincidence?

With aircraft alternating between Westcott and the satellite at nearby Oakley, the first of the Hercules-powered Wellingtons arrived. Previously powered by the Bristol Pegasus engine, the Mk.III and Mk.X versions had the more powerful 1,585 hp V1 radials. The new aircraft allowed 11 OTU to carry out leaflet dropping raids over France, this in turn being very good experience for the crews under training. Known as Operation Nickel, the raids were carried out at night, giving the crews first-hand experience in night navigation and bomb aiming techniques.

Back at Westcott, it was the usual 'Bullseye' exercises with the air gunners getting the opportunity to fire live rounds at a target drogue. On other occasions, Hurricanes were used as targets when the guns were replaced by cine-guns able to record every hit. This of course, compared with live ammunition, was no fun at all!

Staff of No 11 OTU, RAF Westcott 1945. Commanding Officer Group

Though perhaps a little unbelievable in a time of war, Westcott frequently played host to Air Cadets from the local Air Training Corps squadrons. Days, weekends and long summer camps saw the cadets assisting in a number of tasks. Their rewards were usually a flight in a Wellington or an aircraft of the Station Flight, this varying from a Tiger Moth to an Avro Anson. There was certainly no shortage of cadets willing to play their part for at one time during the war, the cadet strength stood at 200,000.

On 9th February 1944, Group Captain Shaw relinquished his command to Group Captain P. Stevens, DFC. He was to be the last commanding officer that Westcott had for by 1944, with the prospect of an assault on Europe, victory was in sight. From this time until 1945, 11 OTU continued to train bomber crews with a

Captain P. Stevens, DFC, is in the centre of the front row. (J Hampton)

peak being reached in March 1945 with 50 Wellingtons on strength together with four Hurricanes and a Miles Master based at Oakley.

By April 1945, the advancing armies on the Continent were beginning to overrun some of the German prisoner of war camps. As they did so, the men were flown home, many of them landing at Westcott and Oakley. For the month of May alone, 20,809 liberated prisoners flew into the former whilst another 15,088 reached Oakley. June saw even more prisoners arrive, a significant day being 2nd June 1945 when 15 Liberators arrived carrying prisoners from Italy. Operation Exodus saw the largest amount of aircraft ever to use the two airfields. Every type was pressed into service including Lancasters, Stirlings and

Halifaxes. During these two months it was not uncommon to see any type of aircraft sitting around the dispersal areas.

The airfield and the local town was decorated with flags and bunting to welcome the men home. They were mainly accommodated in the hangars which had been made more comfortable with the addition of stoves and chairs. By July the majority of prisoners had been returned home and in the same month, Westcott was transferred to 91 Group under whose control it remained until 3rd August when No 11 OTU disbanded.

The airfield was placed under Care and Maintenance until April 1946 when it became the Guided Projectile Establishment, being absorbed into the Royal Aircraft Establishment a year later. Today Westcott is part of Royal Ordnance PLC, a public company which broke from the MOD. Of wartime Westcott, very little remains. Part of the runway and perimeter track is still visible together with several brick and concrete structures. It served its purpose well, and the aircrew that were trained there contributed a great deal to the final victory.

14
WING

In 1931, the Roskill Commission was looking at possible sites in the South East upon which to site London's third airport. Among several suggestions was Cublington in Buckinghamshire, within whose boundary was the former airfield of Wing. Though the site was rejected for various reasons, from 1942 until 1960 Wing served the country well as an Operational Flying Training field. As such, no major events took place there during the war years, which at least showed that the German High Command had their intelligence correct in this instance. However, it is of interest to record the training units and aircraft types that used the airfield.

Surveyed in 1940 as a possible new airfield by the Air Ministry Works Directorate, construction began shortly after. This was finished a year later and on 24th November 1941 an advance party arrived to set up the Station Headquarters. The 2nd December saw the CO, Group Captain J.N.D. Anderson arrive to find the station very basic in its structure. It did however have two hard runways, one running north-south, the other running east-west, a typical layout for a station that was to accommodate large bomber aircraft. Four large 'T' Type hangars and one 'B1' hangar were constructed together with small brick buildings to serve as workshops and offices. From the beginning it was thought that Wing might be prone to enemy attack, this prompting a decoy airfield to be built at Wingrove. Most of the instructional buildings, the Link Trainer and personnel accommodation were built at dispersed sites some distance from the airfield. Air raid shelters were dug and sunk into the grass as well as a gas chamber, bomb dump and incendiary store.

A look at the early diary entries of some of the action that Wing saw explains the use of a station that was really shielded from the worst of the war.

25th April 1941 – No 1 Course began for No 26 OTU. The aircraft complement at this time was eight Ansons with Wellingtons based at the satellite at Cheddington.

11th May 1941 – No 7 Group disbanded, this being replaced by No 92 Group Bomber Command. One of the first operations carried out was for 20 crews to take part in the Cologne 1,000 Bomber raid. The operation cost 26 OTU three crews lost.

10th July 1941 – An air firing flight was formed at Wing with two Wellingtons and one Lysander.

22nd August 1942 – Group Captain Snaith, the Air Ministry overseer for Martin-Baker, arrived to supervise trials of MB3. The MB3 was unique to Wing airfield. It was derived from two previous MB (this standing for Martin-Baker) aircraft, the first of which, MB1, had been test flown at Northolt in 1935. Then a small company, Martin-Baker had a factory at Higher Denham and were at this time engaged on producing a prototype fighter aircraft to Air Ministry specifications. Only one MB1 was built and flown for test purposes but there followed a series of MB aircraft. MB3 was a single seat fighter designed to Air Ministry specification F.18/41. It resembled the North American Mustang of that period and although it was capable of speeds up to 400 mph, only one prototype was built and flown at Wing.

31st August 1942 – MB3-R2492 first flown by Captain H.V. Baker.

12th September 1942 – MB3 destroyed in forced landing following engine failure. Captain Baker killed.

At this point, with the Americans now using Cheddington, Little Horwood became the satellite for Wing. In October, the

Vickers Wellington BX LR132 of No 26 OTU based at Wing and Little Horwood. The Wellington proved the mainstay of all OTUs. (IWM)

aircraft on strength for both airfields were: two Wellington Is, two Wellington IAs, 49 Wellington Cs, six Ansons, three Lysanders, three Tiger Moths, six Defiants and one Proctor. This increased strength gave rise to further operations with bombing raids on German cities such as Dusseldorf and Bremen.

In January 1943, Group Captain J. Bradbury took command of Wing and on 2nd March 1943, two fighter squadrons arrived bringing the sound of the Mustang I to the area. Nos 268 and 613 (City of Manchester) Auxiliary Squadron flew in from Weston Zoyland and Ouston respectively to begin a working up period before changing from Army Co-Operation Command and becoming part of the newly formed 2nd TAF. Both units stayed for seven days before departing to Bottisham.

They were followed on 17th July 1943 by No 1684 (Bomber) Defence Flight from Little Horwood with six Tomahawks. Built by Curtiss in America, the RAF had taken over a quantity of Tomahawks that were intended for the French Air Force. The Tomahawk I first entered service in August 1941, superseding the Lysander in the Army Co-operation role. It further operated in a low level tactical reconnaissance role but whilst at Wing, the aircraft were mainly used for training purposes.

203

Even training airfields had their problems and crashes with fatalities were not uncommon. The 7th August 1942 saw a Wellington III (X3790) airborne from Wing on a training exercise. Carrying a crew of four, it had been instructed to land at Little Horwood. The pilot had just commenced his final approach to the airfield when a red light was seen flashing from the ground. Seeing this, the pilot attempted to overshoot and do another circuit but with his low speed and the fact that his two engines could not give him instant power, he struck the top of some trees. Unable to control the aircraft, it crashed at Winslow in Buckinghamshire destroying several more trees before striking the roof of a house in the High Street. It carried on to demolish the Chandos Arms public house and four other cottages before coming to rest in flames. Sadly, the crew of four and 13 civilians perished in the incident and at an inquest sometime later, it was thought that the pilot under training had lost control through not concentrating on his instruments. The chapters on Little Horwood and Civilians at War give a more in-depth account.

In October, the first consignments of 4,000lb bombs arrived at Wing and Little Horwood. Being an operational flying training base, operations were carried out over enemy territory, as an account of 30th August shows when two Wellington Mk.Xs, and two Mk.IIIs were detailed to bomb a special target in the Forest d'Eperlecques in Northern France. The target was the concrete bunkers which were then producing the fuel for Hitler's revenge weapons, the V1 and V2. One Wellington, HE500, was sadly lost. During the last three months of 1943, the OTU carried out several leaflet dropping sorties, code-named Operation Nickel. Additional sorties were code-named Operation Bullseye, which were night training exercises for bomber and defence personnel.

Being a large airfield with hard runways, Wing was often used by aircraft in distress returning from bombing raids over Germany. The 31st December saw six Boeing B-17s land at the field on return from a raid. Other aircraft that would often be seen sitting around the dispersal areas ranged from Lancasters, Halifaxes and Stirling to smaller fighter types.

Group Captain R.M. Coad assumed command on 1st March 1944 and again an incident on 9th June showed just how dangerous a place a training airfield could be. A Wellington, HE854, had made a bad landing and collided with another Wellington on the ground. This did not stop the aircraft and it further collided with two Queen Mary trailors, one of them carrying a Tomahawk aircraft, and continued its journey finally colliding with No 4 hangar. A major fire developed consuming both aircraft, the trailors and the hangar. The resulting death toll was the three Waaf drivers of No 71 MU and also the co-pilot of the Wellington. It was one of the worst incidents at the airfield.

No 1684 Flight, the Defence Training Flight, was disbanded at Wing on 31st July 1944. Three weeks later, Little Horwood airfield closed down and the personnel were transferred to Wing. However, this was not to be permanent as Little Horwood reopened in October and once again became a satellite to Wing. This again brought the OTU up to full capacity and it is recorded that aircraft on strength were 54 Wellingtons, six Hurricanes and two Magisters.

The last year of the war saw No 60 Group Radar Navigation Aids Test Flight arrive with two Wellingtons. These had been adapted to test the Gee Chain, this being the system used by bombers for accurate navigation. It involved sending synchronised pulses from three stations in Britain which, when picked up by the bombers, enabled the navigator to accurately determine the aircraft's position.

With the imminent end of the war, it is perhaps best to record from the diary once again what part Wing played in the countdown to Victory and for this, I have to thank the historians of Air Britain.

9th April 1945 – Wing became one of several Allied POW repatriation centres in the UK. First batch of 819 men arrived in 33 Dakotas. Further arrivals were on 20th April – 44 Stirlings, 8 Dakotas; 22nd April – 57 Dakotas; 28th April – 5 Dakotas; 14,794 ex-POWs had arrived by 30th April.

May 1945 – Further arrivals included: 4th May – 13 Dakotas, 25 Lancasters; 8th May – 61 Lancasters, 8 Dakotas (1,750 POWs); 10th May – 74 Lancasters; 13th May – 28 Lancasters, 51 Dakotas; 15th May – 132 Lancasters. In all during May, 1,269 aircraft landed at Wing including 621 Dakotas, 518 Lancasters,

The Avro Anson – 'Faithful Annie'. (MAP)

117 Stirlings, 11 Ansons, 1 Hudson and 1 Mitchell. On 10th May, a Lancaster crashed with 31 POWs on board.

15th June 1945 – No 92 Group disbanded; 91 Group took over Wing.

July 1945 – E Flight moved to Wing to become Unit Gunnery Flight.

15th September 1945 – Wing and Little Horwood opened for first Battle of Britain Day.

30th November 1945 – Flying ceased at Little Horwood.

4th March 1946 – No 26 OTU closed. Airfield to Maintenance command on 4th May 1946.

22nd April 1960 – Ground sold by Air Ministry.

So ended the war for Wing. It had served in the Operational Flying Training role admirably and though far from the battle front, had contributed significantly to the war effort.

15
WOODLEY

It was on the outbreak of war that the existing network of Elementary & Reserve Flying Training Schools (E&RFTS) was reorganised. Many schools were closed or amalgamated to form a new training system. These became known as the Elementary Flying Training Schools. One of the larger schools to form was on 3rd September 1939, the day that war broke out. This was No 8 EFTS, which was formed at Woodley near Reading.

A rather small grass airfield, since the mid 1930s it had trained 680 pilots and 108 navigators. The Order of Battle for the RAF in January 1939 stated that Woodley was an airfield in Training Command with its headquarters at Market Drayton in Salop. It was also the base for Reading Royal Air Force Volunteer Reserve whose pilots were trained by the former E&RFTS. Commanded by Wing Commander L.I. Griffiths, the pilots were given initial training at Woodley before progressing to the Flying Training Schools. Though not a fighter station, Woodley was allocated a decoy airfield which was situated at Warfield. It never served its intended purpose for Woodley was not on the enemy hit list. Once the Battle of Britain was over, the decoy was de-requisitioned.

In addition to the EFTS, Miles Aircraft Ltd had established a factory at Woodley before the war. One of their most famous designs and one that served at many of the flying training schools, was the Magister. Known to thousands of RAF pilots who learnt to fly on the type as 'Maggie', it was the first monoplane trainer to be used by the RAF. First delivered to the service in October 1937, it was an all-wooden aircraft derived from the earlier well known series of civil aircraft produced by Mr F.G. Miles and known as the 'Hawks'. Beginning with the Cirrus Hawk of 1932, it included such types as the Hawk Major, Hawk Speed Six and Hawk Trainer. As they rolled out of the Woodley factory, No 8 EFTS became one of the first schools to be equipped with Hawk trainers. Production of the Magister ended in 1941 after 1,203 aircraft had been built, many of them going to the flying training schools such as No 8 at Woodley.

Later designs from the Miles stable were the Miles Master Trainer, first delivered in May 1939 but not nearly as successful as the Magister, and the Miles Martinet, designed as a target tug. In 1943, Miles Aircraft began work on a radio-controlled pilotless version of the Martinet. The original version was superseded by

The basic fighter trainer of 1938/9, made at Woodley airfield – the Miles Magister. (L Pilkington)

the Queen Martinet which reached a production total of 65. All of these aircraft were built, tested and flown from Woodley making it a very important manufacturing airfield. Long before this however, Woodley had witnessed an accident that would change the life of one man and create a Second World War legend.

Monday, 14th December 1931 dawned clear and fine. At RAF Kenley, nestling high on the hills above Caterham in Surrey, the Bristol Bulldogs of No 23 Squadron were lined up in the dispersal area, the early morning sun glinting on their polished aluminium. Two pilots of the squadron, Phillips and Richardson, had arranged to fly to Woodley Aerodrome to see a relation who ran the flying club. They were joined by a third pilot, Flying Officer Douglas Bader, who suggested that he tagged along for the ride. Getting airborne, it did not take long to reach Woodley and all three aircraft landed and taxied up to the clubhouse for coffee and biscuits. Very soon, Bader was engaged in conversation with some of the flying club members who were asking about aerobatics. It was later suggested that he give the flying club a demonstration, but Bader gracefully declined, acting on the orders of his commanding officer back at Kenley. It was just a mild comment of 'windy' from one of the club members that made him change his mind with all the eventual consequences.

Richardson took off first followed by an angry Bader. It was the latter who went directly into an aerobatic routine flying at ground level as he swooped over the clubhouse. It was during one particular manoeuvre that entailed rolling upside down that he felt his aircraft dropping. Attempting to straighten up, his wingtip hit the grass and pulled the Bulldog down to earth. The aircraft crumpled as the engine was torn out of the fuselage. It careered across the grass before coming to a stop.

Bader could feel nothing as his straps continued to hold him tightly in the cockpit. Suddenly all was quiet as he drifted in and out of consciousness. The members of the flying club rushed to help him out as smoke began to come from the crumpled fuselage. As the ambulance arrived, Bader was lifted onto a stretcher and taken to hospital, where he had to come to terms with the loss of both legs. The rest of Douglas Bader's life is a legend and an inspiration to all similarly afflicted. For Woodley, it was the worst accident of any kind that could happen.

The training of pilots continued uninterrupted until 20th July 1942 when No 10 Flying Instructors School took over from No 8 EFTS. Some of the Miles Magisters were exchanged for the venerable Tiger Moth. From this time until the end of the war, training continued apace at Woodley, the amount of flying training giving cause to use Henley as a Relief Landing Ground.

With the war over, Woodley quickly became surplus to RAF requirements and from a busy wartime airfield producing and test flying Miles aircraft, training pilots and repairing damaged aircraft such as Spitfires, it became a part-time base. No 10 FIS survived until 1st June 1945 when it was disbanded.

A few Tiger Moths remained and with these, No 8 EFTS was reformed on 7th May 1946. It had been felt by the Air Ministry that wartime pilots desirous to continue flying, could join the RAF Volunteer Reserve and continue to fly and train at the EFTS. No 8 was instantly retitled No 8 Reserve Flying School. It was equipped with twelve Tiger Moths and two Anson T1s, these being used mainly for refresher flying. The schools were joined

A fine shot of Woodley, the Miles Aircraft Factory and the Miles M.18 prototype. Note the camouflaged hangars. (Crown via B Robertson)

by the Flying Training Command Communications Flight from 1946 until 1951 using a variety of aircraft such as Ansons, Harvards and a Dakota, the personal mount of the C-in-C, Training Command.

Woodley now settled into a peacetime routine. The Tiger Moths were replaced with Chipmunks in 1951, but their use was shortlived as in January 1953 it was announced that seven of the 20 Reserve Flying Schools were to close. Sadly, No 8 RFS was one and it duly disbanded on 31st March 1955. It was the death knell for Woodley for, with Miles Aircraft Ltd ceasing production, all flying stopped. The site fell into disrepair only to be built upon in later years. The airfield had served the nation well, with many aircrew gaining their first introduction to flight at Woodley.

16

THE SMALLER THAMES VALLEY AIRFIELDS

Denham

With its origins in the First World War, Denham in Buckinghamshire is today one of the foremost private flying airfields within the Thames Valley region. Situated south-west of Rickmansworth, from September 1917 until January 1918 it housed Nos 5 and 6 Schools of Military Aeronautics. At the end of the course which consisted of engine engineering, photography and map reading as well as flying training, the pupils were posted to a training depot station with the rank of 2nd Lieutenant. With the armistice however, Denham was closed only to be revived in 1929 when James Martin found the abandoned site. As we have seen in the Heston chapter, he was the co-founder of the Martin-Baker Company. He set up a factory on the site, eventually to occupy over 130,000 square feet of floor area.

The advent of the second conflict brought Denham fully back to life. Two Bellman and two Blister hangars were erected together with limited accommodation. It became a Relief Landing Ground for the Tiger Moths of No 21 EFTS based at nearby Booker. Two grass runways were operational, the north/south being 3,150 feet, north-east/south-west 2,589 feet, east/west 4,150 feet and north-west/south-east 2,400 feet. With these specifications, Denham served as a RLG from 18th November 1941 until 9th July 1945.

With the decline in the flying schools at the end of the war, the field became a base for light aircraft. Today it is a thriving centre for the private flyer with the original east/west runway, 06/24, now asphalt covered. Operated by Bickerton's Aerodromes Ltd, the airfield offers a restaurant and club facilities. All of this a far cry from its wartime usage.

Booker (Wycombe Air Park)

Another of the minor airfields that remain today and has become a centre for light aviation is Booker, sometimes known as Wycombe Air Park. Situated three miles south-west of High Wycombe in Buckinghamshire, it was originally called Marlow Airport.

It came to the notice of the Works Directorate in 1938 and was requisitioned by the Air Ministry in 1939. With the construction of four Bellman hangars and a technical site, Booker became the home of No 21 EFTS. Controlled and operated by Airwork Ltd and encompassed within No 50 Group of Flying Training Command, the usual complement of Tiger Moths arrived supplemented by a few Hawker Harts.

Training began immediately and continued long after the end of the war, eventually disbanding in February 1950. The Korean war brought a new lease of life to Booker when No 1 Basic Flying Training School formed. Again operated by Airwork, the rather more modern De Havilland Chipmunk was used in the training role. Further military usage came when the University of London Air Squadron and the Bomber Command Communications Flight used the airfield and when the military units left, Booker was developed as Wycombe Air Park. Today it continues to flourish as a light aviation centre. The 07/25 runway is asphalt with two further runways remaining grass. The airfield was the venue chosen for the 1975 film *Aces High* when the site was made to resemble an airfield during the First World War and the days of the Red Baron.

213

Feltham/Hanworth Park

When, in 1938, war began to look inevitable, a scheme was introduced whereby impecunious young men, not affiliated to any military body, could have their flying fees paid for by the government by joining an organisation known as the Civil Air Guard. The idea was to stimulate interest in flying and, at minimal cost to public funds, build a cadre of enthusiasts who at least knew the basics of flying. This idea came at a time when many civil flying clubs were finding it difficult to continue due to lack of funding and escalating costs. The Civil Air Guard scheme brought many of them back from the brink of disaster with the generous fees paid by the government.

At Feltham, the London Air Park Flying Club joined the Civil Air Guard during 1938/39. Pupils were issued with a flying overall in RAF blue with silver buttons embossed with the letters CAG. Members of the flying club, on signing an agreement to be available for call up into the RAF in the event of war, would be trained to fly. Having gained a civil pilot's licence, they were allowed ten hours of free solo flying each year, but during training pupils were charged only five shillings per hour with the balance being paid by the government.

Built on a First World War site, the airfield was known by several names. Hanworth Park, London Air Park or Feltham, all referred to the same site. During 1914/18, it was an Aircraft Acceptance Park but the armistice brought a closure of the airfield. It was revived in 1929 when National Flying Services Ltd started to rebuild the site. Several flying clubs were started at Feltham including Flying Training Ltd who occupied a hangar on the north side, and were a subsidiary of Blackburn Aircraft Ltd. The 1st June 1935 saw them form and operate No 5 E&RFTS on behalf of the Air Ministry. They flew Blackburn B2s, Hart trainers, an Anson and a Fairey Battle.

With General Aircraft Ltd, the new owners of the aerodrome, aircraft manufacturing became an important part of the Feltham activities. They themselves were busy building aircraft whilst other companies included the British Aircraft Manufacturing Company Ltd and Rollasons. From this time on the airfield

214

Produced by General Aircraft at Hanworth (London Air Park), the Owlet was used for training purposes for aircraft fitted with a tricycle undercarriage. (Real Life Photos)

became very busy with the Civil Air Guard, No 5 E&RFTS and the manufacturers all jostling for space. On the day that war was declared, No 5 E&RFTS became No 5 EFTS and all civilian flying ceased. No 5 were now re-equipped with the Miles Magister and the newly formed airfield at Heathrow was used as an RLG. It was however, the onset of the enemy bombing during 1940 and the fact that the General Aircraft Company factory received a direct hit from a bomb, that forced No 5 EFTS to move to a quieter area. On 6th June 1940 they moved to Meir near Stoke-on-Trent leaving General Aircraft the sole residents.

Throughout the rest of the war, they remained at Feltham and carried on designing, producing and testing gliders including the Hamilcar and Hotspur. With the cessation of hostilities, they turned their hands to designing a large transport aircraft. Combining their expertise with that of the Blackburn Aircraft Company, they produced the Beverley for the RAF, the prototype being built at Feltham and transported for test flying to Brough.

Today, Feltham remains an airfield although the original clubhouse and hotel is now a retirement home.

Winkfield

Though just a Relief Landing Ground for the Tiger Moths of No 18 EFTS based at Fairoaks, Winkfield in Berkshire served in this capacity from 28th May 1941 until 9th July 1945. It had very few facilities, was just a small grass airfield and saw very little use. Immediately after the war it was de-requisitioned, and today is the site of a radio and space research establishment.

White Waltham

Sometimes known as 'the forgotten pilots', the aircrew that were attached to the Air Transport Auxiliary did a sterling job in delivering a wide variety of aircraft from the manufacturers to the operational squadrons. Their numbers were mainly female and many a bewildered look came across the faces of the squadron pilots when they saw a 'mere slip of a girl' step down from delivering, in some cases, a Halifax or Lancaster. One of the most well known airfields associated with the ATA was White Waltham, situated a few miles south-west of Maidenhead in Berkshire.

Opened on 16th November 1935, it became the home for the second De Havilland School of Flying. Once again the Tiger Moth was the stable mount and when on 18th November 1935, the school became No 13 E&RFTS, no change in aircraft was forthcoming. As with all the other similar units, the school became No 13 EFTS in September 1939. It did not stay very long at White Waltham for in December 1940, it moved to Westwood, a training airfield on the outskirts of Peterborough. Although the airfield was used at various times by the RAF, no operational squadrons were based there during the war.

White Waltham was also home to the ATA Auxiliary Advanced Training School and the ATA Movement Flight. With the end of the war, the need for the ATA diminished, finally being disbanded in 1946. Fairey Aviation immediately used the airfield for testing their Fireflies and Gannets when they moved over from Heston in 1947, and a military presence was continued

The Faithful Annie – an Avro Anson used to transport ATA pilots at White Waltham airfield. (MAP)

when the airfield became the HQ of Home Command. Mosquitos, Ansons, Balliols and Chipmunks now graced the site with further units of the RAF becoming established during the 1950s, including the Home Command Examining Unit. With No 6 Air Experience Flight and Short Brothers forming a first line servicing division, White Waltham, for a period at least, became very busy.

Peacetime however had its drawbacks with the Home Command units leaving in the early 1970s and the Air Experience Flight leaving in 1973. On 31st August of the same year, the airfield closed for military purposes. Once again the civilian flying clubs took it over and it is at this point that we find White Waltham today. Operated by West London Aero Services Ltd, it has full Customs facilities and also has a licensed restaurant and clubhouse.

Smith's Lawn

A private landing strip during the 1930s, Smith's Lawn in Berkshire, in the south-east corner of Windsor Great Park, was selected as a possible site for an airfield. Vickers Armstrong arrived during 1940 and erected a Bellman hangar, eventually starting a production line known as VAXI (Vickers Armstrong Extension 1). Production began of the Wellington Mks V and VI, special high altitude versions of the twin-engined bomber. In addition, the airfield was a RLG for the Tiger Moths of No 18 EFTS based at Fairoaks in Surrey.

Production of the Wellingtons at Smith's Lawn totalled 65 before the end of the war halted all further building. A quantity of Vickers Warwick bombers were stored at the airfield prior to the end and it was also used by an American unit until 1946. Reverting back to its park status in 1947, it is nowadays better known for its sporting activities.

Theale

There is no doubt that the world's most famous training aircraft is the De Havilland Tiger Moth. It remained in service with the RAF for over 15 years and many of them are still flying today in civilian hands. The last biplane trainer in the RAF, it was still being used as a standard elementary trainer as late as 1947 in Flying Training Command and until 1951 with the RAF Volunteer Reserve.

Derived from the Gipsy Moth range of pre-war club aircraft, it differed from the type in having staggered and swept-back wings, this to enable an easier parachute escape from the front cockpit. Ordered by the Air Ministry to Spec.23/31, the prototype first flew on 26th October 1931. By the outbreak of war in 1939, over 1,000 Tiger Moths had been delivered, most of them serving with the Elementary and Reserve Flying Training Schools where RAF pilots were given initial instruction before proceeding to the service flying training schools. The other Air Ministry 'ab initio' training organisations to use the Tiger Moth were the Elementary Flying Training Schools. Theale in Berkshire supported one of these schools for the duration of the war.

Situated some three miles west of Reading and bounded by the Kennet and Avon Canal to the north, the field was requisitioned by the Air Ministry in 1940. Initially it also had been known as

Sheffield Farm and was classed as a Relief Landing Ground to nearby Woodley airfield. It had a rough surface and it was therefore necessary to sow new grass. This took some time before the Ministry found it acceptable. When they did, they authorised the formation of an Elementary Flying Training School to be run under contract by Phillips and Powis Aircraft Ltd. The airfield officially opened on 14th August 1941 and was immediately renamed Theale. It was however, far from complete and a period of heavy rainfall had shown up a considerable water-logging problem.

Two Blister hangars had been erected together with several brick buildings for use as stores or classrooms, but very little airmen's accommodation had been completed. Despite these obvious problems, No 26 EFTS formed at Theale on 21st July 1941 with a complement of 24 Tiger Moths and 60 pupils. The instructors had been posted in from No 8 EFTS but the majority of ground services were handled by civilian personnel under the control of No 50 Group of the RAF. With no buildings complete, the pupils were accommodated in a large country house about a mile from the airfield. Sulhamstead House had been requisitioned for this purpose and was also to act as a school for navigation instruction etc.

The first flying course commenced on 21st August 1941, with the last one finishing on 30th June 1945. The venerable Tiger Moth remained the main type flown but various other types used Theale for communication purposes. Night flying was carried out at White Waltham, there being no facilities at Theale for this type of training. Being an EFTS, there were several major incidents but in the main, Theale had a good safety record.

No 26 EFTS were joined by No 128 Gliding School during 1944. Formed to give Air Cadets experience in gliding, the Slingsby Cadet gliders became as familiar as the Tiger Moths around the local area.

With the end of the war, No 26 EFTS became one of the first to close down. All flying ceased on 30th June 1945. Theale was quickly reduced to Care and Maintenance although 28 Tiger Moths were left sitting around the airfield perimeter awaiting dispersal. The Air Cadets continued to use the facilities until 1948 when the airfield was de-requisitioned and left to an unknown fate. It did not have to wait long before a gravel company moved in and the majority of the site became an enormous pit. Some buildings, including the T1 hangar survived, but the rest have sadly disappeared for ever.

17

CIVILIANS AT WAR

In 1941 in a speech to the nation, Winston Churchill spoke of the risk of a forthcoming invasion. 'A Nazi invasion of Britain last autumn would have been a more or less improvised affair. Hitler took it for granted that when France gave in, we should give in. But we did not give in and he had to think again. An invasion now will be supported by a much more carefully prepared tackle and equipment, landing craft and other apparatus all of which will have been planned and manufactured during the winter months. We must all be prepared to meet gas attacks, parachute attacks and glider attacks with constancy, forethought and practised skill. In order to win the war, Hitler must destroy Great Britain.'

This is just part of one of the many speeches from the Prime Minister that rallied the civilian population. Not for them the ignominious surrender of a nation to Hitler's tyranny. They were defiant in the face of extreme danger and thus, having to suffer the Battle of Britain, the blitz and what followed, the war also became known as a 'people's war'. The words of Neville Chamberlain during 1939 had never convinced the British people that it was 'peace in our time' when they could hear on their wireless the bad news about the rest of Europe. It was obvious that London and the suburbs would be a target when eventually Hitler turned his attention to Britain. The people were not wrong.

Whilst their men were away fighting, the British housewife, left to bring up the children, struggled to cope with rationing, queues and shortages. First introduced in 1940, butter, sugar, bacon and ham were the first to go on ration followed by meat. With these restrictions, the national diet became bread and potatoes and it was deemed a criminal offence to throw any away, however mouldy! Each shopkeeper's supplies were monitored to the amount of registered customers on his or her books and the ration book became the passport to every housewife's budget. The populace were encouraged to turn their flower gardens and lawns into vegetable patches and grow their own produce. The slogan 'Dig for Victory' appeared everywhere, with 'make do and mend' becoming the other 'in' words. The British housewife was certainly encouraged to do her bit.

The passing of the Air Raids Precaution Act in 1937 had brought with it a mass of publications to aid the general public when war eventually came. These included *Air Raid First Aid*, *Rescue Service Manual, First Aid and Nursing for Gas Casualties* and *Protection of your Home against Air Raids*. In addition to the many booklets, the Imperial Tobacco Company issued a set of cigarette cards giving instruction in air raid precautions. Undoubtedly the worst fear of the population was a gas attack, something that in 1939 was thought a distinct possibility. The issue of free respirators or gas masks had an alarming effect on the civilians who thought that a gas attack was imminent. Advised to carry them at all times, the fear wore off during the period of the 'Phoney War' and by the new year of 1940, people had become blase about the whole idea, many declining to carry them at all.

With these new publications came the setting up of Civil Defence Posts for the protection of the people when away from home. Twelve regions were set up with London counting as a single region. By 1939, 1,500,000 civil defence personnel had been recruited, made up of full-time and volunteer wardens. Posts were set up throughout the capital and the suburbs, these being clearly marked and noticeable by the amount of sand-bags surrounding them. During the period of the blitz they would be badly needed. It did not need the Government to tell the people of the country that an invasion could be imminent. They only

Civilians and those engaged in Civil Defence were bombarded with information and government leaflets.

had to listen to the wireless with all the bad news from the Continent and realise that Britain was next on the enemy's list. Everywhere the message was 'don't panic', something easily said but not so easy to carry out (that is of course until the expression became a by-word for a modern-day very popular television series!).

With so many men away on active service, many of those too young or too old, or less able, wanted to do their bit. The opportunity came on Tuesday, 14th May 1940 when the new Secretary of State, Anthony Eden broadcast an appeal.

'I want to speak to you tonight about the form of warfare which the Germans have been employing so extensively against Holland and Belgium. Namely the dropping of troops by parachute behind the main defensive lines. Since the war began, the Government have received countless inquiries from all over

223

the Kingdom from men of all ages who are for one reason or another, not at present engaged in military service and who wish to do something for the defence of their country. Well, now is your opportunity. We want large numbers of such men in Great Britain who are British subjects between the ages of 17 and 65, to come forward now and offer their service in order to make assurance doubly sure. The name of the new force which is to be raised, will be the "Local Defence Volunteers".'

Within 24 hours, 250,000 men had enrolled nationally, this figure rising to more than a million by July. They were not to be known as the LDV for long. In another speech on 23rd July 1940, Winston Churchill referred to the volunteer force as the Home Guard. This name was to be officially adopted immediately after the speech.

One huge problem, however, was equipment. With the regular army needing every piece of equipment for themselves, it fell to the men of the Home Guard to train with a motley collection of impromptu weapons. Many were home-made and were in the extreme, dangerous to handle. Likewise the uniform. Initially issued with LDV and Home Guard arm-bands only, by the summer of 1940, denims became standard issue. Not until mid 1941 was the standard army battledress issued to the units. At the same time, shipments of arms from Canada and America were supplied to the Home Guard, making them at least look as though they meant business!

The main role of the volunteers was to meet the expected invasion by enemy paratroopers and to foil any invasion attempt. Together with evening and weekend training sessions came the guarding of key installations throughout the country. Railways, factories, highways and coastal protection all came under their remit and, even when it became apparent that an invasion was not imminent, the duties remained the same.

As time wore on, the Home Guard did become a well organised disciplined army. Berkshire, Buckinghamshire and Middlesex all had units of the force on regular stand-by. Though the butt of many comedians' jokes, they did much for civilian morale at a very dangerous time. Had an invasion occurred, no doubt they would have given the enemy a run for his money. When the Home Guard was finally stood down in 1944, it was

In the years when our Country

was in mortal danger

FRANK HARWOOD TREWEEKS

who served   20/5/40   to   31/12/44

gave generously of his time and

powers to make himself ready

for her defence by force of arms

and with his life if need be.

George R.I.

THE HOME GUARD

Certificates of thanks were presented to all those who served in the Home Guard. (FH Treweeks) able to hold its head high. No more would the cry be heard, 'Don't panic'!

As well as the Home Guard uniform, civilians were to see many foreign uniforms around their home towns, though in very confined places. A leaflet issued by the Civil Defence in Berkshire during 1940 and headed *Some things you should know if war should come*, covered several buildings and farms requisitioned for the use of prisoners of war. One of the main places was Lodge Farm Camp at Farncombe Down, Lambourn. Very close to the Berkshire/Wiltshire border, it was initially requisitioned as an Italian labour camp but towards the end of the war was considered for Germans. The camp officially opened in August 1941 and was planned to hold 500 prisoners; 120 guards were recruited but this number had to be increased within six months when the camp was expanded to house another 168 men. Further buildings were added but as an experiment, it was decided to house selected Italian POWs in Land Army hostels. These would be under the jurisdiction of the main camp and also under the command of Major R. Fidler, the Commandant. One of the main hostels was situated at Challow in Berkshire with the others based in Wiltshire. Several similar hostels were requisitioned, much to the dismay of the civilian population who did not want enemy POWs in their locality. The main sites in Berkshire were: Winter Quarter's Camp at Ascot (Camp No 7), constructed early in the war; Stratfield Mortimer (Camp No 88), built April 1943; Bradfield Road, Pangbourne, a new hostel built for 70 prisoners during 1943; Brock Hill, Winkfield, a new hostel built for 70 prisoners.

Several other areas of Berkshire were used to aid the war effort including Newbury Racecourse which was used as an American Supply Depot and a camp for Italian and German POWs. All of these sites and many more were included in the Civil Defence leaflet.

In Buckinghamshire, camps for POWs first appeared in 1942, these being for Italians captured in North Africa. Among them was the Hartwell Dog Track near Aylesbury and Shalstone Camp near Buckingham. However, out of the many other camps in the county, it was POW Camp No 300 located at Wilton Park near Beaconsfield that was the most select. Despite, once again,

226

objections from the local people, it was built in 1942 to hold prisoners thought likely to have intelligence information. These included U-boat commanders and German and Italian aircrew. Despite their positions, like the rest of the POWs, they were put to work on the land and in industry. Fraternisation with civilians was strictly forbidden but somehow, some relationships did flourish, even to the extent of the occasional marriage when the war ended.

Whilst prisoners were being sent to POW camps, children were being sent to new homes. It was known as the 'exodus of the innocents' for which there were two main reasons. The fear of bombs and gas was the first whilst the second was more for the control of the civilians by the Government. Believing that when the first bombs began to fall, the population would panic, they felt that an organised evacuation of children initially would prevent this. Friday, 1st September 1939 was the day allocated for the start of the evacuation in the South East for schoolchildren and the elderly sick. Originally 80% of people in London had agreed that their children should be evacuated but as time wore on, only about half were willing to let their children go. However, it was still a huge operation. The first wave of evacuation consisted of 827,000 schoolchildren and 524,000 under school age

With the majority of men in the armed forces, farm boys were recruited to help with the harvest.

accompanied by their mothers. In addition, there were 12,000 expectant mothers and 103,000 teachers and helpers. Carrying a gas mask and a rucksack and labeled with a large card stating name and age, the children were bundled onto trains, buses and coaches and sent to various 'safe' country areas. Some settled into country life quite well, others did not. For many however, it was a brief separation for with the expected bombing not happening until the middle of 1940, three out of four of the evacuees returned home to their mothers and fathers. And most of them stayed, content to put up with the nightly bombing.

For the three counties however, it was not so much a case of sending children away but more of receiving them from London and the South East. All three District Councils had been ordered by the Government to make a house-to-house survey of all available accommodation and to make a return to the Ministry of Health by March 1939. It was found Buckinghamshire could accommodate 116,245 evacuees, Berkshire and Middlesex slightly less. By the time war was declared, Buckinghamshire was receiving evacuees from London. The District Councils in the three counties arranged for the reception of the children and adults in village halls and schools before allocating them to a local family. Some of the children from the poorer areas of London arrived in what was termed a 'verminous condition' and really needed a lot of scrubbing before some families would accept them.

Once settled in a family, one of the greatest problems was the acute overcrowding in schools. Again in Buckinghamshire, the village school at Chilton had to make accommodation for 38 evacuees bringing the total number of children in the school to 108, far too many for a little village. This plus the fact that disagreements between the local children and the evacuees were many made it a very trying time for all, magnified by the extra population moving within the counties. The first evacuees had been moved before the first air raid siren had sounded in anger in London and it was to be many years hence before the last of the evacuees returned home.

Before that however, the Munich Crisis had brought about its own expansion when trenches and shelters were dug and erected all over the country. For people with gardens, the local authorities supplied them with a free Anderson Shelter. Designed by an engineer named Anderson for the Home Secretary, Sir John Anderson (no relation), the instructions for self erection stated that you dug a hole 4 feet wide by 6 feet long, bolted the six pieces of corrugated iron together, tacked on the two end sections and partially covered it in earth or sand. Once erected, people tried to make it as comfortable as possible but one of the main problems was that it was liable to flood in heavy rain. A later shelter that could be used in the house was the Morrison Shelter. This took the form of an iron table with mesh sides for protection from flying bricks or glass should a bomb hit the house. Usually placed in the lounge, it could be used as a table for eating off and as a bed to sleep under. As an infant, yours truly spent many a good night's sleep under such a shelter!

When the bombing of towns and cities began, all three counties were to suffer. The wailing of the sirens forced the civilian population to take cover in whatever way possible. Under the stairs, out to the shelters, down to the underground stations where possible or to the communal shelters provided by the local authorities. In order to convey to the reader the strain that this was to put the civilians under, the following incidents are worth recording and are but a few of the many.

The month of November 1940 saw raids both by day and by night. London and its suburbs were constant targets with attacks on industrial areas, single factories, airfields, civilians and railways. Regarding the latter, an intensive raid in Middlesex on the Southern Railway Thames Valley and Hounslow loop line resulted in the retrieval of an unexploded bomb near Syon Lane station. Although dangerous in the extreme and indicative of many similar incidents, it did have its humour. Without any thought of the bomb exploding when moved, the army managed to defuse it before bundling it onto a railway wheel carriage and dispatching it to be displayed later in aid of the war effort. Such occasions brought a well earned sense of humour to dangerous situations.

Thursday, February 13th/14th 1941. The United Kingdom had cloudy conditions with generally bad visibility. This persisted up until nightfall on the 13th when, with a cloudy and dark night in prospect, no enemy aircraft were expected. This however was not

An all too familiar scene – a building 'well alight' somewhere in southern England. (J Chaffey)

the case for a He 111 of Kampfgeschwader 26. After a journey of some 200 miles from their base at Poix, the crew were heading for their target of the De Havilland aircraft works at Edgware. What they found was a suburb of Hendon.

At around 8.10 pm, they dropped a new type of bomb known as a SC 2500 Max. It fell at West Hendon before any sirens could be sounded to allow people to take to their shelters. It was a densely populated area known as Ravenstone and Borthwick Roads, thus the damage to property was considerable. The blast effect was felt within a quarter of a mile radius, adding to a total of 196 houses destroyed and rendering 170 uninhabitable. A further 400 were damaged, rendering over 600 people homeless from one bomb. It was however the loss of life and the appalling injuries that shook the local community: 75 people lost their lives with another 445 sustaining injuries.

The scale of the death and destruction from one bomb confounded the authorities and caused the Civil Defence to assume that this was indeed, a new type of bomb. A report issued later, however, stated that despite the ferocity of the attack, the spirits of the local people of West Hendon were excellent. All the homeless were soon found temporary accommodation and factory workers in the area turned up for work as usual the next morning. With rescue work continuing until the Sunday evening, a memorial service was held on Sunday, 23rd February on the bombed out site. A make-shift wooden cross surmounted by a wreath was erected as prayers were said and hymns were sung in memory of the dead. Sadly, no cross remains today to mark Hendon's greatest tragedy.

In Newbury, the sirens sounded on 244 occasions with the first on Tuesday, 25th June 1940 at 1.15 am and the last on 29th August 1944. The 'alerts' occupied a period of time amounting to 24,030 minutes with the peak period during the winter of 1940 and the following spring. The town itself experienced three bad bombing attacks, each of which happened on a Wednesday. The first two caused a considerable amount of damage but no deaths. This was to come on the third occasion, the results of which shook the people of Newbury and of Berkshire as a whole.

As 10th February 1943 dawned, the people of the town woke to an overcast day. By midday, the cloud appeared to be lifting and by tea-time, there were definite breaks and signs of blue skies. Being a Wednesday, most of the shops were shut for half day but the town was still busy. At around 4.35 pm, people looked up as the sound of aircraft engines was heard. What they did not see was a lone Dornier 217E of KG40 approaching the town. It was a low level attack which within minutes caused both death and massive destruction to a community. Dropping eight high explosive bombs on the south side of Newbury, St John's church, the senior council school and ten houses were reduced to rubble. Many more buildings close by were damaged, some beyond repair, with many people becoming homeless in minutes. Of greater consequence, however, was the loss of life and terrible

231

Lone Dornier 217Es dropped bombs on Newbury and Reading on 10th February 1943. (MAP)

injuries. Nineteen people perished in the raid with dozens more injured.

The aircraft had approached from the low cloud base over Wash Water. It crossed Monks Lane and Meadow Road, strafing the streets with machine gun fire as it did so. Just over the cemetery in Newton Road, the first bombs fell. Many assumed it was a friendly aircraft and came out of their houses to look up. The first bomb ripped through the houses in Southampton Terrace. It landed in the middle and exploded, killing three women. The second bomb tore through the roof of a building and continued to explode in St John's church, ripping it apart. Fortunately the church was empty with the exception of one of the church workers who was in the vestry at the time. Luckily she escaped with just minor injuries. Further bombs passed through another set of houses in Madeira Place and exploded in a set of almshouses with a terrible loss of life. Another bomb hit the senior council school and whilst luckily most of the children had gone home, three were still on the premises and were killed.

It was Newbury's darkest hour. After the noise of the exploding bombs, for seconds a poignant silence remained until the screams and cries of the dying and injured were heard. Less than a week after the tragedy, a funeral service was held at Shaw cemetery for 13 of the dead, all of them being buried in a communal grave. This was because it had been found impossible to identify certain bodies.

Twenty miles to the east on the same day, another single Dornier bomber again came in fast and low to wreak devastation and death on an innocent civilian population. Like Newbury, in Reading town centre it was early closing day. Despite this, lots of people were out and about in the cold but bright weather. The teashops such as the 'People's Pantry', one of a chain of British Restaurants, were full of customers enjoying a quiet tea. Suddenly, at around 4.35 pm, the quiet was shattered as the staccato sound of machine-gun fire was heard followed by three distinct explosions. This was followed by more gunfire as a Dornier 217 swooped low over the town before climbing away leaving a trail of devastation.

The first bomb had dropped on the Heelas Garage in Minster Street demolishing the premises and those either side of it plus several cars. The second came down on a departmental store which, whilst extensively damaged, incurred no loss of life though several female staff living on the premises were injured. It was however, the third that caused the destruction and many deaths. It fell fairly and squarely on the British Restaurant named the 'People's Pantry'. As the sounds of the first two explosions were heard, many of the customers began to make their way to the door to see what had happened outside. As they did so, the roof fell in as the bomb exploded throwing pieces of red hot metal into flesh and furniture alike. All the customers and staff were instantly buried beneath the rubble of brick and plaster. As the aircraft continued to drop a further bomb next to the church of St Laurence, the noise of its engines and this last explosion helped to block out the cries of the dying and injured.

As the Do 217 continued to climb away, 41 people were left dead with over 100 injured, some very badly. Of the 86 casualties taken to Reading Hospital, one was found dead on arrival, 42 were admitted to the emergency Benyon Ward and the remainder were treated in the casualty department, including Michael Bond, the creator of 'Paddington Bear'. Thirty-one required amputations and six people were so seriously injured that they

Scenes of devastation after a bomb landed on the People's Pantry in Reading on 10.

3, killing and maiming civilians. (Berkshire Chronicle via D Chamberlain)

needed urgent blood transfusions. Three surgeons operated continuously and within seven and a half hours, all the casualties had been dealt with. All the hospital supply of blood had been required and the following day, the donors were recalled and the stock replenished. The search for survivors went long into the night and the next day with the ARP workers toiling to remove debris with their bare hands. They were assisted by all the emergency services but by the afternoon of the next day, all hopes of finding anyone else alive had gone. For one 14 year old who experienced the terror and was badly injured in the attack, it was something he would never forget.

'Wednesday the 10th was cold and at 4.30 I was waiting for a friend who like myself had just left school. We were both due to start work the next week. As he was late at the meeting place, I went next door to a British Restaurant to get a cup of tea to warm me up. These restaurants were set up by the government at the start of the war for war-workers and others to have a cheap meal. Dinner, which comprised of spuds, cabbage and some meat, a pudding, usually sponge, and a cup of tea was only around 1/6d. When I went in there were about 30 people inside. I finished my tea, lit a cigarette and wandered outside walking about 20 yards to the entrance of the arcade which was glass roofed and very old. I didn't hear the sirens sounding but all of a sudden there were three or four explosions and as I looked up, I actually saw a bomb falling. It landed a few yards from where I was standing and as I turned to run, I was blown about 200 yards through the arcade and lay there in the eerie silence.

'Although my ears were ringing, I could still hear the occasional fall of masonry and glass. I cannot remember much after that except waking up in hospital with a fractured skull, broken right femur, broken arm and shrapnel in my back, legs and head. In all I spent eight months in hospital. It really was a bad day for all the people and having researched the incident thoroughly, one person involved was an American serviceman. He was badly injured protecting his English girl-friend and through my research over the years, I was able to go to America in 1996 to meet him once again. I do not think that anyone who was in that attack will ever forget that day.'

Derek Chamberlain was just one of the many injured and was

St Laurence's church, Reading after the Dornier attack. It was the last of a stick of four bombs that caused the damage. (Berkshire Chronicle via D Chamberlain)

indeed lucky that he did not lose his life. For those who did, several of them were buried on Tuesday, 16th February. In a harrowing scene, the remains were interred in the presence of weeping relatives and friends. The early hour chosen had been selected with a view to keeping away sightseers. The bodies were enclosed in coffins of unpolished elm and the graves were draped in purple, floral tributes being placed at the head of each. One grave contained two unidentified bodies and another, the separate coffins of two little children. A large floral cross, composed of carnations, daffodils and arum lilies and inscribed 'From the Corporation, to express the sympathy of the towns-people' was placed on end in the centre. A further cross carried the message, 'as a small tribute from the WVS'.

With the burials over, Reading got back to business. Many people wondered just why such a raid had taken place over a non-military town. Or was it non-military? For 50 years after the event, it was still assumed that the pilot simply picked the town at random to drop his bombs and machine-gun buildings and innocent civilians. No official explanation was forthcoming until 1993 when research revealed that it may not have been a random target. It had been realised early in the war that the high power BBC transmitters would provide radio navigational aids for enemy aircraft. In order to deny the enemy this facility, it was decided that each town with a population of 50,000 or more would receive a low powered transmitter from which to hear the BBC Home Service. Codenamed 'Group H', 61 of these stations were secretly opened with Reading being Station 19. It began operations on 5th May 1941 and it was housed in the 'People's Pantry'. After the war most Group H transmitters were quietly scrapped except a few which were retained for local radio. Was it after all a coincidence that the 'Pantry' received a direct hit or did the German intelligence service excel itself on this occasion?

In Middlesex, many of the buildings situated along the Great West Road supported industries involved in the manufacture of war materials to aid the war effort. Being that much closer to the capital than the neighbouring counties of Berkshire and Buckinghamshire, it was felt that the area would become a target for enemy bombing. Brentford, Chiswick and Isleworth were some of the larger areas thought to be at risk and during the period when the nightly blitz was most intense, did indeed suffer at the enemy's hands. It was however the industrial targets along the Great West Road that attracted the bombs.

One of the first incidents came in December 1940 when the Firestone Tyre works was attacked. Though the attack was severe, the fire watching which most industries practised, gave a forewarning. The workforce was thus able to take shelter before the enemy aircraft were overhead. As they listened and waited in the shelters, the noise above ground became deafening. Four HE bombs were dropped within the area, one of them blowing out the side of the tyre-building shop. With the raid over in as many seconds, the men came out of the shelters to witness carnage. Much of the factory had been razed to the ground with several fires giving off the oily black smoke associated with tyres burning. Several other factories nearby were damaged including such favourites as Smith's Crisps and Macleans Toothpaste. Later in the year, the Great West Road was to be the subject of further attacks by the Luftwaffe with major towns such as Brentford, Harrow, Staines and Enfield all receiving a fair amount of bomb damage.

We have read in the chapters on Little Horwood and Wing of the disastrous crash of a Wellington bomber at Winslow in Buckinghamshire. For two civilians, the incident will forever remain in their memory. Mrs Mavis Dyson was a teenager at the time who kept a diary over most of that period and with her permission I am able to quote from it.

'The war began two months after my 13th birthday. During the previous year there had been much talk of war but to a teenager, this was just 'politicians talk'. However during August 1939, things started to happen. Traffic lights in towns were hooded, gas masks were issued and I can remember just how awful they smelt. The ARP and Home Guard were being formed in towns and villages all over the country but when I tried to join the ARP, I was told I was too young. Then about three days before the 3rd September, the evacuees began to arrive. It seemed as though coach loads of them all arrived at once with helpers and school teachers looking after them. Most of the children looked tired, sad and frightened and when the roll-call had been taken, they were taken to their new homes and foster mums and dads.

Though some distance from the Front Line, Aylesbury did receive substantial bomb damage, as this photo of Walton Road shows. (Bucks CC Library)

'In 1942, the RAF station at Little Horwood was finished and was occupied by No 26 OTU. The coming of the RAF had a wonderful effect on the social life at Winslow and surrounding villages with dances and tea-parties. Apart from all of this, I shall never forget the night that the Wellington bomber crashed into Winslow High Street. I awoke to a dreadful noise and looking out of my bedroom window I could see smoke and fire and could hear shouting everywhere. My dad rushed out of the house and I followed him to see if my granny, who lived just down the road, was alright. When I got there, she was making tea for some of the people so I took over and helped. What had happened was that a bomber had hit a tree, ploughed into a public house and finally come to rest on some cottages. There was the smell of burning petrol hanging over the town for many hours and the damage was dreadful. It was a night that Winslow people would remember for many years as many of them had lost loved ones and friends.'

240

Another Buckinghamshire resident who witnessed the carnage was Bert Shrimpton. Following the incident he recalled that a Court of Inquiry was quickly convened and opened the following Monday. It found that the incident was due to the pilot losing control through not concentrating on his instruments and thus allowing his aircraft to lose height. The Court also found that Flying Control were indirectly to blame in not keeping proper records and allowing aircrew with insufficient experience to participate in night flying exercises unaccompanied. For Mavis and Bert and the many people of Winslow, it was a night they would never forget.

These are but a few incidents among many hundreds that brought death and destruction to the three counties. After the severe bombing came the 'revenge' weapons, the V1 and the V2. Both brought considerable suffering and damage to the area and to an unsuspecting public. Whilst the aiming point for the V1 was the Tower of London, some travelled further and landed in the three counties.

An intact V1 is on display at the Imperial War Museum in London.

Monday, 19th June 1944, six days after the first V1 had been launched, one of the robots came down at Heston. The morning dawned clear but windy. An alert at 06.25 turned out to be a large formation of B-17s outward bound but just before 8 am, a V1 landed in a neat cul-de-sac near Vicarage Farm Road. The owner of one of the houses, Mr Senior, happened to be looking through his kitchen window when he saw the V1 approaching. To his horror he saw the flame from the tail splutter and at the top of his voice shouted, 'That's for us'. Rushing out to the Anderson shelter, he barely made it before the blast from the explosion helped him through the entrance.

Nearby, another neighbour was asleep when the V1 came down. The double bed in which he was sleeping was split down the middle by the blast, with the mattress luckily wrapping itself around him and saving him from personal injury. At the same time, the debris and dust from the roof and ceiling fell into the bedroom. The two occupants of the house together with others made homeless were taken to the Congregational church where their cuts and bruises were attended to. The village hall in Heston was also requisitioned for people made homeless and for the treatment of minor injuries. The rocket, which had landed in the road, caused three deaths with the destruction of almost 1,300 houses around St Leonard's Gardens. A second V1, that came down ten days later in fields at the end of Lampton Avenue, caused only minor casualties and damaged 350 houses as opposed to the first V1. This was because the second rocket came down in a field which absorbed the impact whereas the first exploded on concrete.

Between July and August, three V1s fell on Brentford with the first sadly killing five people. It was however, on 22nd February 1945 that the first V2 fell on the Heston and Isleworth district. A report in the *Daily Herald* dated Saturday, 11th November 1944 said it all on the front page: 'Comets that dive from 70 miles. Britain's front line at home is under fire again from a stratosphere rocket that is dropping on us from 60 to 70 miles up in the air, a rocket that travels faster than sound and flashes across the sky like a "comet trailing fire". There is no warning, no siren, no time to take shelter. For this is the most indiscriminate weapon of this or any other war. It is a sinister, eerie form of war.' Fired high into

A V2 rocket is prepared for flight. (Flight)

the sky, it fell upon the UK with no warning at all.

The first fell beside St Helen's House, completely demolishing the house together with damage to many others. Thirty minor injuries were treated at the local reception centre. It was however, the second V2 to come down within the Heston district that caused the most number of casualties. It fell at 9.39 am on Wednesday, 21st March 1945 onto the Packard engine factory on the Great West Road. Within minutes of the explosion, the rescue services were on the scene but a large fire that was burning at the site prevented any immediate clearance work. This was brought under control with the arrival of the NFS with about 20 vehicles.

The V2 had landed fairly and squarely on the factory, which was producing marine engines. With about 100 men on the shop floor at the time, the entire roof collapsed onto them burying them in brick and corrugated metal. As soon as they were able, the rescue parties moved in and with bare hands, began searching the rubble for survivors. All that day and the next night they toiled until they were sure no one else could have survived. The final toll was 32 killed, 102 seriously injured and 390 slightly injured. Together with Packards, several other factories within the near locality were damaged. A few days after the incident the area was visited by the King and Queen who expressed dismay and sympathy at the dreadful loss of life. They toured the area talking to the workforce and their families and felt the sadness that surrounded the entire area.

These incidents are but a few in what, for the civilian population, was a time of terror. In statistical terms, on 2nd August 1944 Winston Churchill gave a report to Parliament at which he said the total number of V1s, named 'Divers', sent to Britain was then 5,735 which had killed 4,335 people. A later report stated in addition, 1,115 V2s, named 'Big Ben', were fired at Britain which had killed 2,612 people in London alone. There were many others in country areas. Again, according to official records, Berkshire had received two V1 attacks whilst Buckinghamshire received 27. The Middlesex record was possibly incorporated in the London statistics.

Though some distance from the front line, the three counties still suffered a people's war. The memories still linger with the older generation for it was a large part of their lives. They lost

244

fathers, sons, mothers, daughters, sisters and brothers in the conflict and will never forget the time that their particular village or town saw death and destruction.

APPENDIX A

THE SQUADRONS AND UNITS OF THE ROYAL AIR FORCE
AND THE UNITED STATES ARMY AIR FORCE THAT WERE
BASED AT THE THAMES VALLEY AIRFIELDS

BERKSHIRE
ALDERMASTON: Station 467 – 60th TCG, 315th TCG, 370th FG, 434th TCG.
GREENHAM COMMON: Station 486 – 51st TCW, 354th FG, 368th FG, 438th TCG, 316th Group.
GREAT SHEFFORD – RLG for No 8 EFTS.
MEMBURY: Station 466 – 3rd Photographic, 67th Observation Group, 6th Tactical Air Depot, 366th FG, 436th TCG, 525 Squadron RAF, 187 Squadron RAF.
OAKLEY – No 11 OTU.
THEALE – 26 EFTS, 128 Glider Squadron.
WELFORD: Station 474 – 315th TCG, 434th TCG, 435th TCG, 90th TCS, 100th Regional Support Group, 20th FW.
WOODLEY – No 8 E&RFTS, No 8 EFTS, No 10 FIS, No 8 Reserve Flying School.
WINKFIELD – RLG for No 18 EFTS.
WHITE WALTHAM – No 13 E&RFTS, No 13 EFTS, No 3 Ferry Pilots School, No 1 Ferry Pilots School.

BUCKINGHAMSHIRE

BOOKER – No 21 EFTS, No 1 Basic Flying School.

CHEDDINGTON: Station 113 – 44th BG, 12th Combat Crew Replacement Centre, 858th Night Leaflet Squadron, 406th BS, 36th BS.

LITTLE HORWOOD – 26 OTU, 92 Group Communications Flight.

THAME – No 1 Gliding Training Squadron, Royal Naval Air Experiment Department.

WESTCOTT – No 11 OTU.

WING – No 26 OTU, 1684 Bomber Defence Training Flight, No 268 (Chippeway Indian) Squadron RAF, No 613 (City of Manchester) Squadron RAuxAF.

DENHAM – Nos 5 & 6 Schools of Military Aeronautics, RLG for No 21 EFTS.

MIDDLESEX

HENDON – 24, 116, 248, 257, 504, 510, 512, 575, 600, 604, 611.

HESTON – 116, 129, 212, 302, 303, 306, 308, 315, 316, 317, 350, 515.

NORTHOLT – 1, 4, 12, 16, 18, 23, 24, 25, 32, 41, 43, 52, 65, 74, 92, 111, 124, 140, 207, 213, 229, 253, 257, 271, 302, 303, 306, 308, 315, 316, 317, 515, 600, 601, 604, 609, 615.

FELTHAM – 133 Squadron RAF, 155 Squadron RAF.

APPENDIX B

GLOSSARY FOR LUFTWAFFE UNITS

Jagdgeschwader – Fighter Units
Kampfgeschwader – Bomber Units
Zerstorergeschwader – Long Range Fighter Groups
Erprobungs Gruppe 210 – Experimental Test Wing 210
Lehrgeschwader – Instructional/Operational Development
  Group
Stukageschwader – Dive-Bombing Group
Kustenfliegergruppe – Maritime Luftwaffe Units
Kampfgruppe – Coastal Units

GLOSSARY FOR GERMAN AIRCREW RANKS

Oberst (Obst) – Colonel
Oberstleutnant (Obstlt) – Lieutenant Colonel
Major (Maj) – Major
Hauptmann (Hpt) – Captain
Oberleutnant (Oblt) – 1st Lieutenant
Leutnant (Lt) – 2nd Lieutenant
Fahnenjunkeroffizier (Fhnjr) – Officer Cadet
Hauptfeldwebel (Hptfw) – Sergeant Major
Oberfeldwebel (Ofw) – Flight Sergeant
Feldwebel (Fw) – Sergeant
Unteroffizier (Uffz) – Corporal
Flieger (Flg) – Aircraftsman

ACKNOWLEDGEMENTS

I acknowledge with thanks all the individuals and organisations who have assisted me in the writing of this book: Mr Peter Baker; Mr Derek Chamberlain; Mrs Edie Mullins; Miss Pamela Froom; Mr Leonard Lean; Mrs Eileen Snelling; Dr Chris Samson; Mr Len Pilkington; Mr Roger A. Freeman; Mr Cecil G. Curran; Mr Anthony J. King; Mr James Marshall; Hounslow Library Local Studies; Mrs Margaret Carruthers; Mrs Mavis Dyson; Mr Bert Shrimpton; WO J. Wilcox, RAF Northolt; G/Cpt J.J. Witts, DSO, ADC, FRAeS, Commanding Officer, RAF Northolt; *Buckingham Advertiser*; *Bucks Free Press*; *Newbury Weekly News*; Reading Newspaper Series; US Air Force Historical Research Agency; RAF Museum; Imperial War Museum; Air Historical Branch, MOD; Public Records Office, Kew; Mr James Hampton; and special thanks to James Marshall for quoting from his book *The History of the Great West Road*.

If I have omitted to mention any person or organisation or incorrectly credited any photographs, please accept my sincere apologies. Final thanks go to my wife, Barbara, for her patience when spending long evenings alone and for her correcting skills.

BIBLIOGRAPHY

During my research I consulted various other works. I list them below with grateful thanks to the authors.

Ashworth, Chris, *Action Stations 9*, Patrick Stephens 1985.
Bowyer, Chaz, *Fighter Command 1936/68*, Sphere Books 1981.
Bowyer, Michael J.F., *Action Stations 6*, Patrick Stephens 1983.
Chiltern Aviation Society, *From Airships to Concorde*.
Collier, Richard, *Eagle Day*, Pan Books 1968.
Congdon, Philip, *Per Ardua Astra*, Airlife 1987.
Freeman, Roger A., *Airfields of the Eighth*, Battle of Britain Prints Int Ltd 1978.
Freeman, Roger A., *Airfields of the Ninth*, Battle of Britain Prints Int Ltd 1992.
Gardiner, Juliet, *The People's War*, Select Editions 1991.
Halley, James J., *Squadrons of the RAF*, Air Britain 1980.
Halpenny, Bruce Barrymore, *Action Stations 8*, Patrick Stephens 1984.
Jackson, Robert, *Spitfire-The Combat History*, Airlife 1995.
Jefford MBE, W/Cdr C.G., *RAF Squadrons*, Airlife.
Norris, P., *History of Northolt Aerodrome*.
Ramsey, Winston G., *The Battle of Britain Then and Now*, Battle of Britain Prints Int Ltd 1980.
Ramsey, Winston G., *The Blitz – Then and Now*, Battle of Britain Prints Int Ltd 1979.

Rawlings, John, *Fighter Squadrons of the RAF*, MacDonald & Co 1968.

Robinson, Anthony, *RAF Fighter Squadrons in the Battle of Britain*, Brockhampton Press 1987.

Ross DFC, Tony, *75 Eventful Years A Tribute to the RAF*, Wingham Aviation Books 1991.

Smith, David, *Britain's Military Airfields 1939/45*, Patrick Stephens 1989.

Wright, Robert, *Dowding and the Battle of Britain*, Corgi 1970.

INDEX

Squadrons, Units etc

8 EFTS 207, 210, 219
13 EFTS 216
18 EFTS 216, 218
21 EFTS 212, 213
26 EFTS 219
10 FIS 210
2 GTS 52
3 GTS 39
128 GTS 219
11 OTU 174, 178, 196–200
26 OTU 48–49, 107, 111, 202–206, 240
53 OTU 94
61 OTU 94
PDU 91, 92, 93–94
1336 (TS)CU 193
1416 AC Flight 76
1422 ATI Flight 95, 96, 103, 105
1511 BAT Flight 58
1684 BDT Flight 111, 203, 205
92 GC Flight 107, 111
60 GRNAT Flight 205
Special Service Flight 167, 168

USAAF

82nd AD 44, 116, 120
101st AD 39, 43, 61, 115, 116, 120, 185, 186, 187, 191, 192, 193
27th ATG 100

86th ATG 102
10th Aerodrome Sq 102
36th BG 53
44th BG 50, 51
36th BS(H) (RCM) 56
496th BS 54
803rd BS 56
856th BS 53, 56
858th BS 53, 54
325th Ferrying Sq 102
366th FG 114
368th FG 60
370th FG 39
153rd Liaison Sq 113
675th Observation Gp 113
3rd Photographic Gp 113
379th Service Sq 52
39th Service Gp 53
1077th Signal Co 53
9th Station Complement Sq 52
60th TCG 38
315th TCG 39, 40, 185
354th TCG 59, 60
434th TCG 39, 43, 44, 185
435th TCG 185, 187, 191–193
436th TCG 114–121
438th TCG 36, 60–62, 185
51st TCW 58
67th TRG 113
18th Weather Sq 54